What People Are Saying
about *Threshold Bible Study*

"I so appreciate the way Stephen Binz makes the biblical text interesting and accessible to a wide audience without 'dumbing it down.' His passion for Scripture and for upbuilding the faith is admirable!"

 **LAURIE BRINK, OP**, *Professor of New Testament, Catholic Theological Union, Chicago*

"Small groups where men and women of faith can gather to reflect and support each other are essential for the New Evangelization. Stephen Binz has a proven record of supplying excellent resource material to help these groups break open the Scriptures and be nourished and renewed by the living word of God."

ARCHBISHOP PAUL-ANDRE DUROCHER, *Archbishop of Gatineau, Quebec*

"To know and love Jesus and to follow him, we need to know and love the sacred Scriptures. For many years now, the *Threshold Bible Study* has proven to be a vital tool for Catholics seeking to go deeper in their encounter with Christ."

ARCHBISHOP JOSE H. GOMEZ, *Archbishop of Los Angeles*

"*Threshold Bible Study* is a terrific resource for parishes, groups, and individuals who desire to delve more deeply into Scripture and Church teaching. Stephen J. Binz has created guides that are profound yet also accessible and that answer the growing desire among today's laity for tools to grow in both faith and community."

LISA M. HENDEY, *author and founder of CatholicMom.com*

"Stephen Binz provides the Church with a tremendous gift and resource in the *Threshold Bible Study*. This great series invites readers into the world of Scripture with insight, wisdom, and accessibility. This series will help you fall in love with the word of God!"

DANIEL P. HORAN, OFM, *Catholic Theological Union, Chicago*

"*Threshold Bible Study* is by far the best series of short Bible study books available today. I recommend them to all the leaders I help train in the Catholic Bible Institutes of several dioceses. Kudos to Stephen Binz for writing books that are ideal for small-group or individual use."

FELIX JUST, SJ, *Jesuit Biblical Ministries*

"Stephen Binz's *Threshold Bible Study* series gives adults of all ages a very accessible way to 'open wide the Scriptures,' as *Dei Verbum* urged. Encountering the word of God together in study groups will allow participants to deepen their faith and encounter their Savior, Jesus."
■ **ARCHBISHOP JOSEPH E. KURTZ**, *Archbishop of Louisville*

"Inviting, accessible, and wise, *Threshold Bible Study* is an absolutely superb resource for all Catholics interested in unlocking the living word. You now have no excuse not to read and enjoy the Bible."
■ **JAMES MARTIN, SJ**, *author and editor-at-large at America Media*

"Though the distance many feel between the word of God and their everyday lives can be overwhelming, it need not be so. *Threshold Bible Study* is a fine blend of the best of biblical scholarship and a realistic sensitivity to the spiritual journey of the believing Christian. I recommend it highly."
■ **FRANCIS J. MOLONEY, SDB**, *Catholic University of Australia*

"*Threshold Bible Study* is appropriately named, for its commentary and study questions bring people to the threshold of the text and invite them in. The questions guide but do not dominate. Stephen Binz's work stands in the tradition of the biblical renewal movement and brings it back to life."
■ **DR. KATHLEEN M. O'CONNOR**, *Professor Emerita, Columbia Theological Seminary*

"*Threshold Bible Study* takes to heart the summons of the Second Vatican Council—"easy access to sacred Scripture should be provided for all the Christian faithful" (*Dei Verbum*, 22)—by facilitating an encounter with the word of God that is simple, insightful, and engaging. A great resource for the New Evangelization."
■ **DR. HOSFFMAN OSPINO**, *Boston College School of Theology and Ministry*

"The books in the *Threshold Bible Study* series by Stephen J. Binz reflect the ideal Catholic approach to biblical interpretation: sound biblical scholarship, a format accessible for lay readership, and a sensitivity to the Church's life and spirit. This is what the Church means by biblical scholarship at the service of the community of faith."
■ **DONALD SENIOR, CP**, *General Editor of **The Bible Today** and President Emeritus of Catholic Theological Union*

"We are at a unique time in our Church's history when leadership is not confined to a few, but all Catholics are invited to deepen their discipleship and lead in our Church and society. *Threshold Bible Study* helps Catholics reflect on this call in Scripture and put that call into action so that our world may experience the transformation that is possible when we are not simply called Christians but are living and leading in the ways of Christ."
■ **KIM SMOLIK, EdD**, *CEO, Leadership Roundtable*

THRESHOLD
BIBLE STUDY

MUSIC, HYMNS, *and* CANTICLES

Stephen J. Binz

**TWENTY-THIRD
PUBLICATIONS**
twentythirdpublications.com

TWENTY-THIRD PUBLICATIONS
977 Hartford Turnpike, Unit A
Waterford, CT 06385
(860) 437-3012 or (800) 321-0411
www.twentythirdpublications.com

ISBN: 978-1-62785-704-8
Printed in the U.S.A.

 A division of Bayard, Inc.

Contents

LESSONS 13–18

LESSONS 19–24

LESSONS 25–30

How to Use
Threshold Bible Study

Each book in the *Threshold Bible Study* series is designed to lead you through a new doorway of biblical awareness, to accompany you across a unique threshold of understanding. The characters, places, and images that you encounter in each of these topical studies will help you explore fresh dimensions of your faith and discover richer insights for your spiritual life.

Threshold Bible Study covers biblical themes in depth in a short amount of time. Unlike more traditional Bible studies that treat a biblical book or series of books, *Threshold Bible Study* aims to address specific topics within the entire Bible. The goal is not for you to comprehend everything about each passage but rather for you to understand what a variety of passages from different books of the Bible reveals about the topic of each study.

Threshold Bible Study offers you an opportunity to explore the entire Bible from the viewpoint of a variety of different themes. The commentary that follows each biblical passage launches your reflection about that passage and helps you begin to see its significance within the context of your contemporary experience. The questions following the commentary challenge you to understand the passage more fully and apply it to your own life. The prayer starter helps conclude your study by integrating learning into your relationship with God.

These studies are designed for maximum flexibility. Each study is presented in a workbook format, with sections for reading, reflecting, writing, discussing, and praying. Space for writing after each question is ideal for personal study and allows group members to prepare in advance for their discussion. The thirty lessons in each topic may be used by an individual over the period of a month, or by a group for six sessions, with lessons to be studied each week before the next group meeting. These studies are ideal for Bible study groups, small Christian communities, adult faith formation, student groups, Sunday school, neighborhood groups, and family reading, as well as for individual learning.

The method of *Threshold Bible Study* is rooted in the classical tradition of *lectio divina*, an ancient yet contemporary means for reading the Scriptures reflectively and prayerfully. Reading and interpreting the text (*lectio*) is followed by reflective meditation on its message (*meditatio*). This reading and reflecting flows into prayer from the heart (*oratio* and *contemplatio*).

This ancient method assures us that Bible study is a matter of both the mind and the heart. It is not just an intellectual exercise to learn more and be able to discuss the Bible with others. It is, more importantly, a transforming experience. Reflecting on God's word, guided by the Holy Spirit, illumines the mind with wisdom and stirs the heart with zeal.

Following the personal Bible study, *Threshold Bible Study* offers a method for extending *lectio divina* into a weekly conversation with a small group. This communal experience will allow participants to enhance their appreciation of the message and build up a spiritual community (*collatio*). The end result will be to increase not only individual faith but also faithful witness in the context of daily life (*operatio*).

Through the spiritual disciplines of Scripture reading, study, reflection, conversation, and prayer, you will experience God's grace more abundantly as your life is rooted more deeply in Christ. The risen Jesus said: "Listen! I am standing at the door, knocking; if you hear my voice and open the door, I will come in to you and eat with you, and you with me" (Rev 3:20). Listen to the Word of God, open the door, and cross the threshold to an unimaginable dwelling with God!

SUGGESTIONS FOR INDIVIDUAL STUDY

- Make your Bible reading a time of prayer. Ask for God's guidance as you read the Scriptures.

- Try to study daily, or as often as possible according to the circumstances of your life.

- Read the Bible passage carefully, trying to understand both its meaning and its personal application as you read. Some persons find it helpful to read the passage aloud.

- Read the passage in another Bible translation. Each version adds to your understanding of the original text.

- Allow the commentary to help you comprehend and apply the scriptural text. The commentary is only a beginning, not the last word, on the meaning of the passage.

- After reflecting on each question, write out your responses. The very act of writing will help you clarify your thoughts, bring new insights, and amplify your understanding.

- As you reflect on your answers, think about how you can live God's word in the context of your daily life.

- Conclude each daily lesson by reading the prayer and continuing with your own prayer from the heart.

- Make sure your reflections and prayers are matters of both the mind and the heart. A true encounter with God's word is always a transforming experience.

- Choose a word or a phrase from the lesson to carry with you throughout the day as a reminder of your encounter with God's life-changing word.

- For additional insights and affirmation, share your learning experience with at least one other person whom you trust. The ideal way to share learning is in a small group that meets regularly.

SUGGESTIONS FOR GROUP STUDY

- Meet regularly; weekly is ideal. Try to be on time and make attendance a high priority for the sake of the group. The average group meets for about an hour.

- Open each session with a prepared prayer, a song, or a reflection. Find some appropriate way to bring the group from the workaday world into a sacred time of graced sharing.

- If you have not been together before, name tags are very helpful as a group begins to become acquainted with the other group members.

- Spend the first session getting acquainted with one another, reading the Introduction aloud, and discussing the questions that follow.

- Appoint a group facilitator to provide guidance to the discussion. The role of facilitator may rotate among members each week. The facilitator simply keeps the discussion on track; each person shares responsibility for the group. There is no need for the facilitator to be a trained teacher.

- Try to study the six lessons on your own during the week. When you have done your own reflection and written your own answers, you will be better prepared to discuss the six scriptural lessons with the group. If you have not had an opportunity to study the passages during the week, meet with the group anyway to share support and insights.

- Participate in the discussion as much as you are able, offering your thoughts, insights, feelings, and decisions. You learn by sharing with others the fruits of your study.

- Be careful not to dominate the discussion. It is important that everyone in the group be offered an equal opportunity to share the results of their work. Try to link what you say to the comments of others so that the group remains on the topic.

- When discussing your own personal thoughts or feelings, use "I" language. Be as personal and honest as appropriate and be very cautious about giving advice to others.

- Listen attentively to the other members of the group so as to learn from their insights. The words of the Bible affect each person in a different way, so a group provides a wealth of understanding for each member.

- Don't fear silence. Silence in a group is as important as silence in personal study. It allows individuals time to listen to the voice of God's Spirit and the opportunity to form their thoughts before they speak.

- Solicit several responses for each question. The thoughts of different people will build on the answers of others and will lead to deeper insights for all.

- Don't fear controversy. Differences of opinions are a sign of a healthy and honest group. If you cannot resolve an issue, continue on, agreeing to disagree. There is probably some truth in each viewpoint.

- Discuss the questions that seem most important for the group. There is no need to cover all the questions in the group session.

- Realize that some questions about the Bible cannot be resolved, even by experts. Don't get stuck on some issue for which there are no clear answers.

- Whatever is said in the group is said in confidence and should be regarded as such.

- Pray as a group in whatever way feels comfortable. Pray for the members of your group throughout the week.

Schedule for Group Study

SESSION 1: INTRODUCTION   DATE: _____

SESSION 2: LESSONS 1–6   DATE: _____

SESSION 3: LESSONS 7–12   DATE: _____

SESSION 4: LESSONS 13–18   DATE: _____

SESSION 5: LESSONS 19–24   DATE: _____

SESSION 6: LESSONS 25–30   DATE: _____

"Be filled with the Spirit, as you sing psalms and hymns and spiritual songs among yourselves, singing and making melody to the Lord in your hearts." EPHESIANS 5:18–19

Music, Hymns, and Canticles

Long before human beings began creating music and song, the natural world was doing what it was created to do—praising God with its own musical sounds and melody. Singing birds, chirping tree frogs, whistling wind, rolling thunder, the rhythm of waves—all creating a symphony of beauty and blessing.

From their earliest origins, humans have imitated the sounds around them and used their ingenuity to create new ones. Mimicking the cadence of nature, people began snapping their fingers, clicking their tongues, clapping their hands, and slapping their stomachs with the flat of their hands. Exhausting the noisemaking possibilities of their own bodies, they began hitting sticks together, drumming on a log, and tapping on a stretched animal skin. The movement of wind through trees and canyons gave rise to various sounds made with breath passing through the mouth and lips. This led to the sounds made by blowing through animal horns and the invention of pipes and reed instruments. Later a greater range of melody was made possible through the development of stringed instruments. Once animal gut was strung on a bow for hunting, the twang produced when the arrow took flight suggested the tonal possibilities that led to the lute and the lyre.

As humanity developed language, songs emerged as words were combined with the tenor provided by the human voice and the melody produced

1

by musical instruments. The variety of songs became as wide as the variety of human activities. Lullabies were sung to soothe a child or agitated flocks. Daily labor was accompanied by musical chants to absorb the monotony and maintain the rhythm of the work. The transitional events of life were marked with music and song: the merrymaking of weddings, the thanksgiving songs of new birth, and the dirges of funerals. Songs rallied troops for battles; then victories were celebrated and defeats were lamented. Festivals, feasts, processions, and observances of every kind were accompanied by music and dancing. The range of emotions expressed through music was anything but limited. Songs expressed a great variety of moods and feelings: joy and sorrow, faith and doubt, gratitude and vengeance, hope and fear.

Humanity realizes that its most important music should be directed in praise to the Lord who gave music to the world. There is something instinctual within human communities that seek to lift their voice in song to the divine, and sacred music has forever issued forth from the lips of people worshipping their gods. This study will focus on the music that developed within the community of ancient Israel and the early Christian church, the song and melody that has been preserved for us in the Old and New Testaments.

Reflection and discussion

- What is the music of the natural world that you hear during the day? During the night?

- What are your earliest memories of music and song?

Music in Ancient Israel

In every stage of Israel's history and every facet of life for God's people, music has played a central role. Because Israel's prohibitions against images prevented them from developing a tradition of visual arts, the Israelites developed a robust oral and aural culture, emphasizing speech and sound. For this reason, music was an especially important aspect of life. From the least to the greatest, the people of the Bible sang and played musical instruments.

Among the most ancient words in the Hebrew Scriptures are sung texts in connection with victories in battle and the veneration of heroes. The Song of the Sea and Song of Miriam commemorate God's victory over Pharaoh of Egypt (Exod 15), the Song of Deborah celebrates the defeat of Israel's Canaanite adversaries (Judg 5), and singing and dancing honor the victories of David over the Philistines (1 Sam 18:6–7).

In the early chapters of Genesis, which serve as a prologue for Israel's history, Jubal is said to be "the ancestor of all those who play the lyre and pipe." He is mentioned alongside the first to breed and raise livestock and the first smith, who made tools of bronze and iron (Gen 4:20–22). These legendary ancestors show the essential nature of music and its embeddedness in the daily life of God's people.

Since the Israelites engaged in a mixture of pastoral and agricultural activities, planting, harvesting, and sheepshearing were occasions for festive gatherings and religious celebrations. The young women of Shiloh danced each year beside their vineyards (Judg 21:19–21), and the sons of David celebrated a feast following the shearing of Absalom's sheep (2 Sam 13:23–28). The wedding ritual included a meeting between the bride and the groom's party, accompanied by musicians playing tambourines (1 Macc 9.37–39).

David brought the ark of the covenant up to Jerusalem amidst great rejoicing. A procession led into the city, while David and the people sang and danced to the sound of musical instruments (2 Sam 6:5). The coronation of kings was announced with the sounding of trumpets and a procession led into Jerusalem to the tune of pipes (1 Kgs 1:39–40). A group of "royal psalms," commemorating the dynasty of David, were sung at royal festivals (Pss 2, 20, 72, 89, 101, 110, 144). An annual feast acclaiming the enthronement of God was marked by a grand procession to the temple, "the singers in front, the musicians last, between them girls playing tambourines" (Ps 68:25).

The people of Israel always remembered David as the God-anointed singer and composer of Israel's psalms. Yet David himself claims that it is God who inspired his compositions: "He put a new song in my mouth" (Ps 40:3), and "The spirit of the Lord speaks through me" (2 Sam 23:2). David is present in the psalms in a number of ways. Some of them sing about his reign, God's covenant with him, and the divine promises given to him. Other psalms are marked "of David," a phrase that many understand to mean that David wrote them. Still others contain notations that associate them with events in David's life. Some of the royal psalms may have even been composed for his coronation, and others relate either directly or indirectly to his reign. Undoubtedly David wrote some of the psalms, while in a more general sense his legacy inspired those who wrote the rest. He is the guiding voice of the entire Book of Psalms, and his spirit sings in every one of them.

Other occasions for music making in ancient Israel were pilgrimages to sacred shrines like Shiloh and Bethel. After the construction of the temple in Jerusalem, pilgrimages were centered on the capital city for the annual feasts of Passover, Weeks, and Booths, bringing thousands of people streaming to the city. Pilgrim songs were an important part of the journey, especially the "psalms of ascent," providing opportunities for cheerfulness and melodious prayer along the way (Pss 120—134).

The music of worship gained a formal, liturgical setting at Jerusalem's temple as professional guilds of musicians were employed to form choirs and orchestras. These singers from among the Levites were tasked with performing the music for the calendar of religious events at the temple. Called to "prophesy with lyres, harps, and cymbals," they were obligated to give God constant praise, perform the epic songs of God's past victories, and execute the rituals for the annual cycles of religious feasts (1 Chron 25). Each guild was responsible for a particular repertoire of songs, which aided in preserving this music during periods of war and exile.

Although professional groups of musicians provided the dominant song and musical accompaniment for temple worship, the congregation was never excluded from the ritual sounds of the temple. The *Shema* (Deut 6:4–9) and other familiar words could have been chanted in unison by the whole assembly. Many other texts throughout the Bible suggest how people would have sung familiar refrains throughout the music. For example, in Psalm 136, the continual refrain, "for his steadfast love endures forever," would have been rhythmically chanted by the assembly. Other psalms suggest that the people's response, "Praise the Lord" and "Hallelujah" was added to the song of the guilds (Pss 148—150).

Given the rich beauty and joy of Israel's music, it is no wonder that the refusal to play instruments and sing became the most poignant way of expressing the people's desolation as they were marched away into exile: "By the rivers of Babylon—there we sat down and there we wept when we remembered Zion. On the willows there we hung up our harps. For there our captors asked us for songs, and our tormentors asked for mirth, saying, 'Sing us one of the songs of Zion!' How could we sing the Lord's song in a foreign land?" (Ps 137:1-4). This refusal to sing at the taunt of their tormentors shows that music expressed a spontaneous and irrepressible outpouring of emotion, not something that can be beckoned with external manipulation.

After the exile in Babylon, those returning to Jerusalem included "two hundred male and female singers" (Ezra 2:65). As the new foundation of the Lord's temple was laid, the ceremony was marked by the priests in their vestments praising God with trumpets and the levitical guilds playing cymbals, while all sang responsively, "praising and giving thanks to the Lord, for he is good, for his steadfast love endures forever toward Israel" (Ezra 3:10-11).

Reflection and discussion

- Why did the Israelites refuse to sing the "songs of Zion" while exiled in Babylon?

• How could my reading of Old Testament texts be enhanced by imagining the sounds of music that pervade the scenes?

Music in the Early Church

Since the first followers of Jesus worshiped in the temple and the synagogues of Judaism, the emerging music of Christianity was most influenced by these contexts from which it arose. After the glorification of Jesus, his followers continued to chant the psalms and other lyrical texts of the Scriptures of Israel. Christianity inherited its appreciation for the biblical word from its roots in ancient Israel and Judaism. So Christian music at its core is vocal music that serves the Scriptures.

While there is no indication that musical instruments were banned from early Christian assemblies, simple chant predominated. Attending a performance of music, listening to it for its own sake, was relatively unknown in early Christianity. As in other cultures of the ancient Near East, music was woven into the fabric of community living and public worship.

In Christian homes, simple blessings were chanted over meals, and psalms were sung throughout the day, making these homes mostly indistinguishable from Jewish households. Assemblies of worship also took place typically in larger homes. Paul urged his communities to make music an integral aspect of their new life in Christ, to be filled with the Spirit, and to sing "psalms and hymns and spiritual songs" to the Lord with joy and gratitude (Col 3:16; Eph 5:19). Lyrical fragments from Judaism, such as "Hosanna," "Amen," "Alleluia," and "Maranatha," naturally also became Christian expressions and took on a Christ-centered usage. As time passed, the Jewish texts and melodies of the early believers began to be reshaped with Jesus Christ at their heart, offering a more enlarged and distinctive repertoire of prayers, songs, and melodies.

Although the New Testament does not contain as many musical texts as the Scriptures of Israel, it offers sufficient indications to let us know that music was indispensable for both daily life and worship. Short, lyrical formulas of praise are found throughout the New Testament, like the doxology sung by the angels at the birth of Jesus: "Glory to God in the highest heaven, and on earth peace among those whom he favors" (Luke 2:14). In time, these Jewish texts led to the development of doxologies centered on Christ: "To the only wise God, through Jesus Christ, to whom be the glory forever!" (Rom 16:27).

As Christians chanted their prayers of praise, they directed them to God and "in the name of" or "through" Jesus. In other texts, singing is directed "to the Lord," most likely to the exalted Jesus Christ. In the letters of Paul, Christ is both the one to whom worship is offered, as he is included in the identity of God, and also the one through whom worship is offered. A similar development is seen in Hebrews. Its opening verses are a lyrical text exalting Christ as the "heir of all things" and as worthy of the worship due to God: "He is the reflection of God's glory and the exact imprint of God's very being, and he sustains all things by his powerful word" (Heb 1:3). Yet, at the same time, his is the leader of the congregation's song addressed to God: "I will proclaim your name to my brothers and sisters, in the midst of the congregation I will praise you" (Heb 2:12).

Developing Christian texts expressed an increasingly trinitarian dynamic of worship. The personal presence of God the Spirit initiates and sustains the church's prayerful singing. Through Christ we have "access in one Spirit to the Father" and become "members of the household of God" (Eph 2:18–19). This trinitarian dynamic of worship becomes the dynamic of redemption. The Spirit unites us to Christ and him to us, so that with him, as well as through him, we have access to the Father.

Larger musical texts of the New Testament include the canticles of Luke's infancy accounts, which have been set to music from the first century until today. These texts also contain hymns to Christ sung within the early Christian communities and included within the letters of Paul and Peter. Christian hymns and canticles were incorporated within New Testament writings destined for the urban Gentile world of the empire, indicating that Christians carried their embrace of the musical heritage of Judaism into the larger world of Greco-Roman culture.

God's redeemed people "sing to the Lord a new song" (Isa 42:10). In the New Testament, this motif is incorporated into the Book of Revelation, expressing what music means to the biblical imagination. All in the heavenly assembly "sing a new song" before the divine throne and before the sacrificed and glorified Lamb (Rev 5:9; 14:3). The visionary hears "the sound of harpists playing on their harps" (Rev 14:2) and trumpets announcing the time of judgment and redemption. Most pervasive of all is the sound of singing as the saints in heaven praise God for their salvation.

Reflection and discussion

- What is the role of the Holy Spirit in the music of the New Testament?

- How is the liturgical music of today similar to and dissimilar from the music of the early church?

The Sound of Music in the Bible

Biblical studies, archeology, and musicology tell us a great deal about the significance of music in the biblical period and its importance for the secular and sacred life of ancient people. Yet the texts give us no musical notes and few directions, so we don't know exactly how the music of the Bible sounded.

In the ancient world there was no clear distinction between speaking and singing. The lyrical character of speech, especially when offering praise or prayer, encompassed melodic features that drifted toward song. Especially when poetic texts were recited with the accompaniment of musical instruments, the text could certainly be labeled a hymn or canticle. Because the Bible presents a God who communicates primarily through the word, the auditory environment of worship held many sound shadings between speech and music.

The music in biblical times generally took the form of a single line of notes, without any harmony or counterpoint. It was free of any strict metered rhythm and followed the patterns and rhythms of speech far more closely than music today. We know that songs were often sung as a simple chant, but on other occasions the performance was quite exuberant. Psalm 150, for example, presents a veritable symphony of sound in praise of God. It calls for blasts of trumpets and rejoicing with lute and harp, tambourine and dance, strings and pipes, and even the sound of crashing cymbals. But the exact melodies performed by voices and instruments alike have not come down to us.

Music was a primary tool for preserving the history and truths of God's people through the ages. Long before the Scriptures were committed to writing by scribes, the stories of people's experiences of God were preserved in oral poetry and song, each generation performing these stories for the next generation. The poetic speech and songs enshrined in the writings of Scripture tell us in countless ways that the one, true, and holy Lord delivered his people. Whatever their anguish, oppression, or need, they experienced God's presence with them in the bond of covenant. A common melody flows throughout all the music of ancient Israel and the church of Jesus, the melody of divine love, calling, pursuing, delivering, and redeeming the people God has chosen to be his own.

We can be grateful that we have no record of what, precisely, the psalms, hymns, and canticles of the Bible sounded like when performed. This void has spurred the artistic imaginations of liturgical composers throughout the ages. Just as much of the music of ancient Israel centered on worship at the shrines and temple, music in the Christian period developed around the eucharistic liturgy. Indeed, the scriptural roots of music for the Christian liturgy take us back to the Last Supper. In the gospels we read that, after the Passover meal, Jesus and the gathered community of disciples sang a hymn (Matt 26:30; Mark 14:26). Although the hymn is not specified, Jewish norms for Passover called for singing the Hallel, a song of praise and thanksgiving corresponding to the verses of Psalms 114 to 118.

In the venerable Hallel, we hear echoes of the first song of the Bible, with which Moses and the Israelites celebrated their liberation from Egypt. It praises God's name, offers thanksgiving for his gifts, and extols his greatness beyond all idols and nations. Toward the end of the Hallel (Ps 118:25–26) we find the Hebrew cry of "Hosanna!" (Save us, Lord) along with the acclamation "Blessed is the one who comes in the name of the Lord." These continue to be sung in the eucharistic liturgy today. It is moving to ponder what Jesus might have felt as he sang these very words.

As we study the music, hymns, and canticles of the Bible, let us consider that Jesus sang many of these himself as he was raised in the tradition of ancient Israel. And let us heed the words of Paul in his letter to the Colossians: "Let the word of Christ dwell in you richly; teach and admonish one another in all wisdom; and with gratitude in your hearts sing psalms, hymns, and spiritual songs to God. And whatever you do, in word or deed, do everything in the name of the Lord Jesus, giving thanks to God the Father through him (Col 3:16–17).

Reflection and discussion

- Why is music and song the easiest way to keep the history of a people alive from age to age?

- How do I desire the Holy Spirit to work in me during this study?

Prayer

Lord our God, the source and the goal of all human creativity, send your Holy Spirit to guide, encourage, and enlighten me as I begin this study of the music in your inspired Scriptures. I praise you for the ways you enable your children to make music to express the emotions of the heart. During this study, help me to appreciate the music, hymns, and canticles of ancient Israel and the early church, and teach me how to lift my voice to give you praise and thanks.

SUGGESTIONS FOR FACILITATORS, GROUP SESSION 1

1. If the group is meeting for the first time, or if there are newcomers joining the group, it is helpful to provide name tags.

2. Distribute the books to the members of the group.

3. You may want to ask the participants to introduce themselves and tell the group a bit about themselves.

4. Ask one or more of these introductory questions:
    - What drew you to join this group?
    - What is your biggest fear in beginning this Bible study?
    - How is beginning this study like a "threshold" for you?

5. You may want to pray this prayer as a group:
    Come upon us, Holy Spirit, to enlighten and guide us as we begin this study of the music and songs of Scripture. You inspired the biblical authors to express your word as manifested to the people of Israel and most fully in the life of Jesus. Motivate us each day to read the Scriptures and deepen our understanding and love for these sacred texts. Bless us during this session and throughout the coming week with the fire of your love.

6. Read the Introduction aloud, pausing at each question for discussion. Group members may wish to write the insights of the group as each question is discussed. Encourage several members of the group to respond to each question.

7. Don't feel compelled to finish the complete Introduction during the session. It is better to allow sufficient time to talk about the questions raised than to rush to the end. Group members may read any remaining sections on their own after the group meeting.

8. Instruct group members to read the first six lessons on their own during the six days before the next group meeting. They should write out their own answers to the questions as preparation for next week's group discussion.

9. Fill in the date for each group meeting under "Schedule for Group Study."

10. Conclude by praying aloud together the prayer at the end of the Introduction.

Then the prophet Miriam, Aaron's sister, took a tambourine in her hand; and all the women went out after her with tambourines and with dancing. EXODUS 15:20

Song of the Sea and Song of Miriam

EXODUS 15:1–21 *¹Then Moses and the Israelites sang this song to the Lord:*
"I will sing to the Lord, for he has triumphed gloriously;
    horse and rider he has thrown into the sea.
²The Lord is my strength and my might,
    and he has become my salvation;
this is my God, and I will praise him,
    my father's God, and I will exalt him.
³The Lord is a warrior;
    the Lord is his name.
⁴"Pharaoh's chariots and his army he cast into the sea;
    his picked officers were sunk in the Red Sea.
⁵The floods covered them;
    they went down into the depths like a stone.
⁶Your right hand, O Lord, glorious in power—
    your right hand, O Lord, shattered the enemy.
⁷In the greatness of your majesty you overthrew your adversaries;
    you sent out your fury, it consumed them like stubble.
⁸At the blast of your nostrils the waters piled up,
    the floods stood up in a heap;
    the deeps congealed in the heart of the sea.

[9]*The enemy said, 'I will pursue, I will overtake,*
I will divide the spoil, my desire shall have its fill of them.
I will draw my sword, my hand shall destroy them.'
[10]*You blew with your wind, the sea covered them;*
they sank like lead in the mighty waters.
[11]*"Who is like you, O Lord, among the gods?*
Who is like you, majestic in holiness,
awesome in splendor, doing wonders?
[12]*You stretched out your right hand,*
the earth swallowed them.
[13]*"In your steadfast love you led the people whom you redeemed;*
you guided them by your strength to your holy abode.
[14]*The peoples heard, they trembled;*
pangs seized the inhabitants of Philistia.
[15]*Then the chiefs of Edom were dismayed;*
trembling seized the leaders of Moab;
all the inhabitants of Canaan melted away.
[16]*Terror and dread fell upon them;*
by the might of your arm, they became still as a stone
until your people, O Lord, passed by,
until the people whom you acquired passed by.
[17]*You brought them in and planted them on the mountain*
of your own possession,
the place, O Lord, that you made your abode,
the sanctuary, O Lord, that your hands have established.
[18]*The Lord will reign forever and ever."*
[19]*When the horses of Pharaoh with his chariots and his chariot drivers went into the sea, the Lord brought back the waters of the sea upon them; but the Israelites walked through the sea on dry ground.*

[20]*Then the prophet Miriam, Aaron's sister, took a tambourine in her hand; and all the women went out after her with tambourines and with dancing.* [21]*And Miriam sang to them:*
"Sing to the Lord, for he has triumphed gloriously;
horse and rider he has thrown into the sea."

A lthough the verb "to sing" and the noun "song" are found hundreds of times throughout the Bible, this first mention sounds the basic theme for the rest: praising God for salvation. This first biblical song makes its appearance in quite dramatic fashion. Having escaped from Egypt, the sea parts and the Israelites are delivered, definitively, from slavery by the power of God. In response, Moses and the Israelites sing "to the Lord," recounting their deliverance and pondering its significance (verse 1).

The song is not a celebration of the Egyptians' defeat but of the Lord's victory. The stanzas of the song are performed to bring honor to the Lord. The song begins with the words "he has triumphed gloriously," and they end with "The Lord will reign forever and ever" (verse 18). The praise and thanksgiving given to God serve as a witness about God before all the world. Peoples beyond the Israelites may be drawn to the Lord as God's reputation reverberates throughout the earth.

The first section of the song focuses on the experience of the Israelites at the sea (verses 2–12). As witness to divine deliverance, it focuses on the Lord: "my strength," "my salvation," and "my God." The singers bear testimony to the saving power God provided by intervening at the sea. As a "warrior," God defeated the advancing army of the Egyptians for a people who had no army of their own (verse 3). Pharaoh's chariots, his army, and his elite officers were cast into the sea where they sank like a stone (verses 4–5).

The song interprets the saving events in cosmic terms, emphasizing their universal effects. The episode at the sea is a particular episode of God's worldwide purposes of setting straight a chaotic world. God's "right hand," the glorious power of the Creator God, is continually at work destroying all those forces opposed to life and freedom: crushing injustice, overcoming domination, and vanquishing oppression. The Lord's fiery fury consumed the enemy like stubble, and his powerful wrath lifted high mountains of water (verses 6–8). When the pride of the enemy boasted, God blew the wind, the sea covered them, and they sank like lead (verse 9–10). In a triad of praise, the singers express the incredible deliverance they have experienced: "Who is like you, O Lord, among the gods? Who is like you, majestic in holiness, awesome in splendor, doing wonders?" (verse 11).

The second section of the song shifts the focus away from the victory at the sea and looks forward to the journey ahead (verses 13–18). The "holy abode," the mountain sanctuary to which God led the Israelites, is the land of God's promise and, ultimately, Jerusalem, the site of God's temple on Mount Zion. The people and leaders of Philistia, Edom, Moab, and Canaan panicked in terror as God's chosen ones passed by. The Lord brought them to their goal, and there he will reign over them forever.

Miriam the prophet, the sister of Moses, then enters the scene with the other Israelite women (verses 20–21). They joyfully play the tambourine and dance to the music. Miriam's Song is the refrain with which the Song of the Sea began, except Moses' singular "I will sing to the Lord" is replaced by the plural imperative of Miriam, [Let us all] "sing to the Lord." The two songs work together to provide verses and refrain, call and response. Miriam and all the women lead the singing and dancing in celebration of God's great victory.

Reflection and discussion

- What indicates that this song is not about Israel's victory or Egypt's defeat? Who is the true victor in this hymn?

- What shows me that this song is not just about a historical event, but also about God's bringing order from chaos and victory over the forces of oppression? How might it be performed in later victory processions in Jerusalem?

Prayer

Victorious God, you have triumphed gloriously in overthrowing the oppressors and bringing your people to freedom. You who are majestic in holiness and awesome in splendor, lead your people to your holy abode, where you reign forever.

As an eagle stirs up its nest, and hovers over its young; as it spreads its wings, takes them up, and bears them aloft on its pinions, the Lord alone guided him. DEUTERONOMY 32:11–12

The Song of Moses

DEUTERONOMY 31:19–22, 30; 32:1–12 ¹⁹*Now therefore write this song, and teach it to the Israelites; put it in their mouths, in order that this song may be a witness for me against the Israelites.* ²⁰*For when I have brought them into the land flowing with milk and honey, which I promised on oath to their ancestors, and they have eaten their fill and grown fat, they will turn to other gods and serve them, despising me and breaking my covenant.* ²¹*And when many terrible troubles come upon them, this song will confront them as a witness, because it will not be lost from the mouths of their descendants. For I know what they are inclined to do even now, before I have brought them into the land that I promised them on oath."* ²²*That very day Moses wrote this song and taught it to the Israelites.*

³⁰*Then Moses recited the words of this song, to the very end, in the hearing of the whole assembly of Israel:*

32 ¹*Give ear, O heavens, and I will speak;*
    let the earth hear the words of my mouth.
²*May my teaching drop like the rain,*
    my speech condense like the dew;
like gentle rain on grass,
    like showers on new growth.
³*For I will proclaim the name of the Lord;*
    ascribe greatness to our God!

⁴*The Rock, his work is perfect,*
    and all his ways are just.
A faithful God, without deceit,
    just and upright is he;
⁵*yet his degenerate children have dealt falsely with him,*
    a perverse and crooked generation.
⁶*Do you thus repay the Lord,*
    O foolish and senseless people?
Is not he your father, who created you,
    who made you and established you?
⁷*Remember the days of old,*
    consider the years long past;
ask your father, and he will inform you;
    your elders, and they will tell you.
⁸*When the Most High apportioned the nations,*
    when he divided humankind,
he fixed the boundaries of the peoples
    according to the number of the gods;
⁹*the Lord's own portion was his people,*
    Jacob his allotted share.
¹⁰*He sustained him in a desert land,*
    in a howling wilderness waste;
he shielded him, cared for him,
    guarded him as the apple of his eye.
¹¹*As an eagle stirs up its nest,*
    and hovers over its young;
as it spreads its wings, takes them up,
    and bears them aloft on its pinions,
¹²*the Lord alone guided him;*
    no foreign god was with him.

Toward the end of Israel's Torah, as the life of Moses is about to end and the people prepare to cross into the promised land, God instructs Moses to write a song—the best memory device in the ancient world, as it is today—and teach it to the Israelites (verses 19–22). If the covenant between God and Israel is to have a future, it must lie in the fidelity of God and not in the obedience of his people. As they enter the fruitful land and enjoy its benefits, they will sing this song in praise of God, whose trustworthiness will outshine all the failures of historical Israel and ultimately be acknowledged by all the nations.

The song of Moses opens with a call to the heavens and the earth to pay attention to this valuable presentation on the nature of God (verses 1–3). It expresses the hope that these lyrics will be received as eagerly as the rain is welcomed and have the same life-giving effect. For the singer "will proclaim the name of the Lord," announcing God's greatness in dealing with his people.

The song begins to draw a sharp contrast between the perfection of God and the deficiencies of his people (verses 4–5). Describing God as "the Rock," the text emphasizes the Lord's stability and permanence, stressing the unchanging nature of the God of the covenant. But Israel, unlike its Rock, is corrupt, stubborn, and deceitful. The deficiencies of God's people are all the more stark in comparison with the Lord's dealings with them (verse 6). In their foolishness, they failed to recognize him as their father, the one who formed and established them as his own people. To reject that grace and covenant love by acting with infidelity was tantamount to discarding their very reason for being.

The call to "remember the days of old" is an invitation to reflect on Israel's past history and to inquire about its meaning from the previous generations (verses 7–9). God's actions in the past are of continuing significance for the present and future of his people. God is called "the Most High," sovereign over the whole world. He divided the whole earth among many nations and even gave them their own gods, yet the Lord took only Jacob (Israel) as his own people.

With poetic imagery, the song describes God's care for his people in the wilderness (verses 10–12). He guided, protected, nourished, and supported them in that dangerous land. The image of an eagle taking care of its young conveys the continual providence of God. As the eagle trains its young to fly, stirring them from the nest and carrying them on its wings, God led Israel through the perils of its young life. Since no other god has guided their history, no other god has any claim on their worship.

Reflection and discussion

- Why is God described as Israel's Rock (verse 4)? As their father (verse 6)?

- What aspects of God are conveyed through the image of an eagle?

- Is it more difficult to follow God in times of prosperity or in times of adversity?

Prayer

Most High God of all the earth, unchanging in your ways and constant in your care, you are the refuge and protector of your people. Be my steady source of confidence in storms and trials, my anchor in a tottering world.

"Hear, O kings; give ear, O princes; to the Lord I will sing, I will make melody to the Lord, the God of Israel." JUDGES 5:3

The Song of Deborah

JUDGES 5:1–13, 19–31 ¹*Then Deborah and Barak son of Abinoam sang on that day, saying:*

²*"When locks are long in Israel,*
when the people offer themselves willingly—
bless the Lord!

³*"Hear, O kings; give ear, O princes;*
to the Lord I will sing,
I will make melody to the Lord, the God of Israel.

⁴*"Lord, when you went out from Seir,*
when you marched from the region of Edom,
the earth trembled,
and the heavens poured,
the clouds indeed poured water.

⁵*The mountains quaked before the Lord, the One of Sinai,*
before the Lord, the God of Israel.

⁶*"In the days of Shamgar son of Anath,*
in the days of Jael, caravans ceased
and travelers kept to the byways.

⁷*The peasantry prospered in Israel,*
they grew fat on plunder,
because you arose, Deborah,
arose as a mother in Israel.

⁸*When new gods were chosen,*
then war was in the gates.
Was shield or spear to be seen
among forty thousand in Israel?
⁹*My heart goes out to the commanders of Israel*
who offered themselves willingly among the people.
Bless the Lord.
¹⁰*"Tell of it, you who ride on white donkeys,*
you who sit on rich carpets
and you who walk by the way.
¹¹*To the sound of musicians at the watering places,*
there they repeat the triumphs of the Lord,
the triumphs of his peasantry in Israel.
"Then down to the gates marched the people of the Lord.
¹²*"Awake, awake, Deborah!*
Awake, awake, utter a song!
Arise, Barak, lead away your captives,
O son of Abinoam.
¹³*Then down marched the remnant of the noble;*
the people of the Lord marched down for him against the mighty.

¹⁹*"The kings came, they fought;*
then fought the kings of Canaan,
at Taanach, by the waters of Megiddo;
they got no spoils of silver.
²⁰*The stars fought from heaven,*
from their courses they fought against Sisera.
²¹*The torrent Kishon swept them away,*
the onrushing torrent, the torrent Kishon.
March on, my soul, with might!
²²*"Then loud beat the horses' hoofs*
with the galloping, galloping of his steeds.
²³*"Curse Meroz, says the angel of the Lord,*
curse bitterly its inhabitants,
because they did not come to the help of the Lord,

to the help of the Lord against the mighty.
²⁴"Most blessed of women be Jael,
   the wife of Heber the Kenite,
   of tent-dwelling women most blessed.
²⁵He asked water and she gave him milk,
   she brought him curds in a lordly bowl.
²⁶She put her hand to the tent peg
   and her right hand to the workmen's mallet;
she struck Sisera a blow,
   she crushed his head,
   she shattered and pierced his temple.
²⁷He sank, he fell,
   he lay still at her feet;
at her feet he sank, he fell;
   where he sank, there he fell dead.
²⁸"Out of the window she peered,
   the mother of Sisera gazed through the lattice:
'Why is his chariot so long in coming?
   Why tarry the hoofbeats of his chariots?'
²⁹Her wisest ladies make answer,
   indeed, she answers the question herself:
³⁰'Are they not finding and dividing the spoil?—
   A girl or two for every man;
spoil of dyed stuffs for Sisera,
   spoil of dyed stuffs embroidered,
   two pieces of dyed work embroidered for my neck as spoil?'
³¹"So perish all your enemies, O Lord!
   But may your friends be like the sun as it rises in its might."
And the land had rest forty years.

This ancient victory song is one of the oldest literary witnesses to Israel's life prior to the monarchy. As poetry, it offers an impressionistic glimpse—in lyric, image, rhythm, and wordplay—into the tribal existence of God's people. The victorious battle celebrated by the song is narrated in the chapter of prose that precedes it (Judg 4). Deborah, a prophetess and judge, serves as both legal counsel and military strategist. She has called upon Barak, a military commander, to lead the battle against the Canaanite general, Sisera. Barak agrees to command the troops, but only if Deborah goes with him into battle against the Canaanite troops with their nine hundred iron chariots (Judg 4:8, 13).

Deborah desires all the kings and princes of the earth, far and near, then and in succeeding generations, to "hear" of the wonderful works God has done for his people. So she will "sing" and "make melody" to the Lord (verse 3). The hymn displays God's sovereignty on a cosmic scale, as the cause of Israel's miraculous victory on that memorable day. As God "marched" from Edom in stormy power, "the earth trembled," "the heavens poured" down rain, "the clouds indeed poured water," and "the mountains quaked" (verses 4–5). As "the One of Sinai," the Lord has dominion over the waters: regulating the waters of the sea when he led Israel to freedom from the Egyptians and directing the waters of the heavens to pour down rain when he saved Israel from the Canaanites.

Before telling the story of God's wondrous deliverance, the singer gives an impression of Israel's life before Deborah arose. The Canaanites controlled the roads and trade routes, so "caravans ceased and travelers kept to the byways" (verse 6). But when Deborah attained leadership, she became known as "a mother in Israel," nurturing and revitalizing the life of the people (verse 7). Because the Israelites have rejected their covenant with the Lord and chosen other gods, war came upon this weakened people, without shield or spear for defense (verse 8).

Then the call to battle is sounded and many "offered themselves willingly," from the richest to the poorest—those who ride on donkeys, sit on rich carpets, and walk by the way (verses 9–10). The musicians at the village wells sing of the Lord's past triumphs, and those who respond to the call assemble at the city gates (verse 11). As Deborah and Barak hearten the troops, the battle is fought against the Canaanite kings and their general, Sisera. The heavens joined in the fight, and the Canaanite troops and their dreaded chariots are overwhelmed by the storm and resulting flash flood (verses 19–23). Horse and rider are swept away and drowned, echoing the victory caused by the rising waters remembered in the Song of the Sea (Exod 15:1, 4–5, 8). The victors rejoice, while those who refused to offer themselves for battle are cursed.

Sisera escaped from the battlefield and sought safety in the tent of Jael, a Canaanite woman who is honored in song as "most blessed of women" (verses 24–27; Judg 4:17–22). Offering rest to the enemy's general, she completes the victory for Israel in the least likely way. The song expresses the death of Sisera with exquisite language: the beat of the horses' hoofs is echoed by the sound of the mallet striking the tent peg into the head of the general. His death at the feet of Jael highlights the unexpected ways that God works to defeat the enemies of his people. Such startling assistance will forever encourage the Israelites to trust God in seemingly impossible circumstances.

The final verses of the song shift the spotlight to another woman, "the mother of Sisera," standing at the window of her palace, waiting for her son to return on his chariot from battle (verses 28–30). Her ladies comfort her by reminding her of the spoils of war that the commanders must be dividing among themselves. She thinks of the beautifully embroidered garments Sisera will bring to her. Lest the picture of a mother waiting for her son who would never return home should evoke sympathy from the hearer of the song, her gleeful expectation of the Canaanite men raping the Israelite women should stifle any such pity.

What began with Deborah, "a mother in Israel," ends with a mother in Canaan—one victorious and one vanquished. Deborah sings her canticle of victory, while the mother of Sisera must sing a mourner's lament. God has brought down the proud and lifted up the lowly. The divine reversal is complete. God's enemies perish, while the Lord's friends—Deborah, Barak, Jael, and the people who offer themselves willingly—rise like the sun (verse 31).

Reflection and discussion

- What are the similarities between this Song of Deborah and the Song of the Sea?

- How does Deborah's song inspire trust in future generations of God's people?

- Why are the images of the two mothers so strikingly contrasted in this song?

- How may the message of this song be summarized in the words of Paul in 2 Corinthians 12:9–10?

Prayer

God of Israel, there is no hope of deliverance apart from you, the Source of life and salvation. Keep me faithful to my covenant commitments so that I may rise like the sun and offer myself willingly for the work of your kingdom.

He raises up the poor from the dust; he lifts the needy from the ash heap, to make them sit with princes and inherit a seat of honor. 1 SAMUEL 2:8

Hannah Rejoices in the Lord

1 SAMUEL 2:1–10 *¹Hannah prayed and said,*
"My heart exults in the Lord;
my strength is exalted in my God.
My mouth derides my enemies,
because I rejoice in my victory.
²There is no Holy One like the Lord,
no one besides you;
there is no Rock like our God.
³Talk no more so very proudly,
let not arrogance come from your mouth;
for the Lord is a God of knowledge,
and by him actions are weighed.
⁴The bows of the mighty are broken,
but the feeble gird on strength.
⁵Those who were full have hired themselves out for bread,
but those who were hungry are fat with spoil.
The barren has borne seven,
but she who has many children is forlorn.
⁶The Lord kills and brings to life;
he brings down to Sheol and raises up.

⁷*The Lord makes poor and makes rich;*
  he brings low, he also exalts.
⁸*He raises up the poor from the dust;*
  he lifts the needy from the ash heap,
to make them sit with princes
  and inherit a seat of honor.
For the pillars of the earth are the Lord's,
  and on them he has set the world.
⁹*"He will guard the feet of his faithful ones,*
  but the wicked shall be cut off in darkness;
  for not by might does one prevail.
¹⁰*The Lord! His adversaries shall be shattered;*
  the Most High will thunder in heaven.
The Lord will judge the ends of the earth;
  he will give strength to his king,
  and exalt the power of his anointed."

Hannah, the childless but favored wife of Elkanah, had withstood years of ridicule and contempt because of her barrenness. Her longing for a child and her plea to the Lord to look favorably upon her is narrated in the preceding chapter (1 Sam 1). While on pilgrimage at Shiloh, Hannah poured out her heart to the Lord and promised that if God would give her a son, she would give him back to God. Confident in her prayers and the blessing of Eli the priest, Hannah conceived and bore a son named Samuel. Then after several years, she returned to Shiloh to present her son for the Lord's service.

When Hannah came to the shrine, she brought her son, her sacrifice, and this song. Whether her prayerful chant was her own composition or a known hymn that she chose to use on this occasion is unknown and irrelevant. But the fact that the author of the books of Samuel chose this song as the overture to this story of Israel is most significant. For in this canticle of Hannah, we have a reflection on the power of God and the powerlessness of human beings. It introduces the narrative of the books of Samuel, which moves from the oppressed and powerless people we see in Judges to the liberated and unified nation that God provided through the reign of King David. It is also remarkable that this overture is chanted by a woman, one who had been barren and powerless but is now raised and empowered by God.

The song begins with Hannah's rejoicing in God with all her heart and strength (verse 1). Through the birth of her child, Hannah's worth and dignity have been restored. But this unforeseen birth is understood to be more than a personal, familial occurrence. It is an affirmation that concerns God's whole people. Like the womb of Hannah, the future of Israel has been opened to new possibilities. If a son is given in the midst of barrenness, what other prospects might God create for this troubled people? Israel sings with Hannah in praise and hope.

Because God understands and judges all human actions, the proud and haughty are deposed in favor of those who are humble (verse 3). Here begins a series of reversals proclaiming how God humbles the arrogant and lifts up the lowly. Those who have been so well off for so long now lose what they most valued: strong warriors are defeated while the weak gain strength; the satiated become hungry while the famished have their fill; the barren gives birth to a family while the mother of many is forsaken (verses 4–5).

God, who is sovereign even over matters of war, food, and children, determines even matters of life and death (verse 6). Those who are poor and powerless, seated in the ash heap, are given seats of honor (verses 7–8). God, who has set the earth on pillars to prevent it from sinking into chaos, controls the world and will take care of his faithful people. Human strength is of no avail, and opposition to God will lead to disaster (verses 9–10). Finally, God will raise up his king and provide the anointed one with his own strength and authority.

Hannah joins her voice with the music Israel has been singing since its liberation from Egypt. The tradition of Samuel, into which this song has been inserted, moves from the newly arrived child to his work as God's instrument in choosing David as king. Indeed there is new hope for lowly Israel because of its holy, powerful, and steadfast God.

Reflection and discussion

- Why is it significant that this prayer is chanted by the mother of Samuel?

- What other stories of the Bible speak of lifting up the lowly and bringing down the mighty?

- When has God brought me from a place of barrenness to new hope for the future?

Prayer

Holy One of Israel, there is no one besides you, bringing down the arrogant and mighty, while lifting up the humble and lowly. Teach me to trust in you in all circumstances of my life, and give me hope in a glorious future.

Whenever the evil spirit from God came upon Saul, David took the lyre and played it with his hand, and Saul would be relieved and feel better, and the evil spirit would depart from him. 1 SAMUEL 16:23

David Plays the Lyre for Saul

1 SAMUEL 16:14–23 ¹⁴*Now the spirit of the Lord departed from Saul, and an evil spirit from the Lord tormented him.* ¹⁵*And Saul's servants said to him, "See now, an evil spirit from God is tormenting you.* ¹⁶*Let our lord now command the servants who attend you to look for someone who is skillful in playing the lyre; and when the evil spirit from God is upon you, he will play it, and you will feel better."* ¹⁷*So Saul said to his servants, "Provide for me someone who can play well, and bring him to me."* ¹⁸*One of the young men answered, "I have seen a son of Jesse the Bethlehemite who is skillful in playing, a man of valor, a warrior, prudent in speech, and a man of good presence; and the Lord is with him."* ¹⁹*So Saul sent messengers to Jesse, and said, "Send me your son David who is with the sheep."* ²⁰*Jesse took a donkey loaded with bread, a skin of wine, and a kid, and sent them by his son David to Saul.* ²¹*And David came to Saul, and entered his service. Saul loved him greatly, and he became his armor-bearer.* ²²*Saul sent to Jesse, saying, "Let David remain in my service, for he has found favor in my sight."* ²³*And whenever the evil spirit from God came upon Saul, David took the lyre and played it with his hand, and Saul would be relieved and feel better, and the evil spirit would depart from him.*

1 SAMUEL 18:6–16 ⁶*As they were coming home, when David returned from killing the Philistine, the women came out of all the towns of Israel, singing and*

30

dancing, to meet King Saul, with tambourines, with songs of joy, and with musical instruments. ⁷*And the women sang to one another as they made merry,*

> *"Saul has killed his thousands,*
> *and David his ten thousands."*

⁸*Saul was very angry, for this saying displeased him. He said, "They have ascribed to David ten thousands, and to me they have ascribed thousands; what more can he have but the kingdom?"* ⁹*So Saul eyed David from that day on.*

¹⁰*The next day an evil spirit from God rushed upon Saul, and he raved within his house, while David was playing the lyre, as he did day by day. Saul had his spear in his hand;* ¹¹*and Saul threw the spear, for he thought, "I will pin David to the wall." But David eluded him twice.*

¹²*Saul was afraid of David, because the Lord was with him but had departed from Saul.* ¹³*So Saul removed him from his presence, and made him a commander of a thousand; and David marched out and came in, leading the army.* ¹⁴*David had success in all his undertakings; for the Lord was with him.* ¹⁵*When Saul saw that he had great success, he stood in awe of him.* ¹⁶*But all Israel and Judah loved David; for it was he who marched out and came in leading them.*

David rose from life as a shepherd in the fields of Bethlehem to be anointed as the greatest king of ancient Israel. Chosen by God among the eight sons of Jesse, David's life spanned from the simplicity of a shepherd's hillside to the opulence of a royal palace. It pleased God to raise him from his lowly estate and set him on Israel's throne.

As he grazed his sheep in the fields, a talented young musician emerged from this solitary life. David's early life was inseparable from the sounds of nature, the music of the lyre, and the simple songs that became the basis for the music David composed later in his life. He was truly, as Samuel declared of him, "a man after [God's] own heart" (1 Sam 13:14). Unlike Saul, who became king because the Israelites insisted on having a king, David was God's own choice to rule over his people.

As these vignettes make clear, music, hymns, and canticles were woven throughout David's life. The first account of David's musical skills shows him being recruited to provide soothing music to ease what is called King Saul's "evil spirit," a mental illness characterized by bouts of depressive moods.

Eager to find relief for his affliction and discovering that David is "skillful in playing the lyre," Saul ordered Jesse to send his son David to serve in his palace.

We can imagine David playing his lyre for Saul and singing psalms to soothe the anxiety and fears associated with the king's troubled state of mind (16:23). David's therapeutic skills led the king to become deeply attached to the handsome young musician. David remained in the king's service, becoming his armor-bearer and trusted confidant.

When Saul and David were returning home after the defeat of the Philistines, the women of the villages welcome the king and his men with joyful singing and dancing, playing tambourines and other musical instruments (18:6–7). Although their victory song appropriately honors Saul as the royal leader and David as his warrior, with Saul killing thousands and David ten thousands, Saul becomes increasingly jealous and suspicious of David.

The next day, while David was playing the lyre for Saul, the king raved and threw his spear at David (18:10–11). In his desperation, Saul sends David away from the court and into the field to command the army, which only made David more visible and popular with the people and a greater threat to Saul (18:12–14). The whole kingdom grew in their affection for David, while Saul increasingly feared that both human and divine support would be taken from him and given to David.

Reflection and discussion

- In what ways do I experience the therapeutic power of music?

- In what ways is the life of David characterized by music and song?

- What besides music can bring relief and healing to a troubled conscience and an anxious heart?

- In what ways do one's own self-doubts and insecurity cause jealousy toward others?

- How can I bring comfort and peace to those experiencing tension and anxiety?

Prayer

Lord, make me an instrument of your peace for those afflicted in mind and body, who need to experience confidence and hope. Help me be compassionate when others experience failure and rejoice when others achieve success.

David and all the house of Israel were dancing before the Lord with all their might, with songs and lyres and harps and tambourines and castanets and cymbals. 2 SAMUEL 6:5

David in Lamentation and Jubilation

2 SAMUEL 1:17–27 ¹⁷*David intoned this lamentation over Saul and his son Jonathan.* ¹⁸*(He ordered that The Song of the Bow be taught to the people of Judah; it is written in the Book of Jashar.) He said:*

¹⁹*Your glory, O Israel, lies slain upon your high places!*
  How the mighty have fallen!
²⁰*Tell it not in Gath,*
  proclaim it not in the streets of Ashkelon;
or the daughters of the Philistines will rejoice,
  the daughters of the uncircumcised will exult.
²¹*You mountains of Gilboa,*
  let there be no dew or rain upon you,
  nor bounteous fields!
For there the shield of the mighty was defiled,
  the shield of Saul, anointed with oil no more.
²²*From the blood of the slain,*
  from the fat of the mighty,
the bow of Jonathan did not turn back,
  nor the sword of Saul return empty.
²³*Saul and Jonathan, beloved and lovely!*
  In life and in death they were not divided;

they were swifter than eagles,
  they were stronger than lions.
²⁴*O daughters of Israel, weep over Saul,*
  who clothed you with crimson, in luxury,
  who put ornaments of gold on your apparel.
²⁵*How the mighty have fallen*
  in the midst of the battle!
Jonathan lies slain upon your high places.
  ²⁶*I am distressed for you, my brother Jonathan;*
greatly beloved were you to me;
  your love to me was wonderful,
  passing the love of women.
²⁷*How the mighty have fallen,*
  and the weapons of war perished!

2 SAMUEL 6:1–5 ¹*David again gathered all the chosen men of Israel, thirty thousand.* ²*David and all the people with him set out and went from Baale-judah, to bring up from there the ark of God, which is called by the name of the Lord of hosts who is enthroned on the cherubim.* ³*They carried the ark of God on a new cart, and brought it out of the house of Abinadab, which was on the hill. Uzzah and Ahio, the sons of Abinadab, were driving the new cart 4with the ark of God; and Ahio went in front of the ark.* ⁵*David and all the house of Israel were dancing before the Lord with all their might, with songs and lyres and harps and tambourines and castanets and cymbals.*

Although the musical legacy of David is most often associated with the Book of Psalms, several of his songs can be found in the Bible's narrative books. Since David was a skilled leader with a heart of courage and compassion, he won strategic military battles, brought peace to warring tribes, and resolved political disputes. Yet he always bowed before God and praised him for his victories and sang in thanksgiving for God's unending faithfulness.

Following the death of Saul and his son Jonathan in battle David composed and sang a lament. "The Song of the Bow" became a memorial hymn sung in honor of the slain heroes and written in the Book of Jashar, a lost collection of Israel's poetry (verses 17–18). David's grief is heartfelt and personal, since he lived with Saul for so long and loved Jonathan so deeply, but his lament is also an expression of the nation's public grief. Whether the damage is personal or communal, where loss is not honestly grieved there are barriers to renewal.

The slaughter of Israel's army and the death of its king and prince were an utter tragedy for those left behind. Israel's splendor has been lost in this moment of defeat (verse 19). "How the mighty have fallen!" is the powerful refrain that will be reiterated again. David expresses the unrealistic hope that the news not be spread to the Philistine cities of Gath and Ashkelon, where it will only become a subject of mockery (verse 20). The daughters of the Philistines will rejoice while the daughters of Israel weep. The mourning is so great that even the land must share it (verse 21). It is inconceivable that the mountains of Gilboa should continue yielding crops when Israel's anointed king had been slain on their slopes.

The lament takes us into the clash of battle, where the relentless "bow of Jonathan" spilled "the blood of the slain" and the mighty "sword of Saul" cut "the fat of the mighty" (verse 22). The king and his son died together, united in purpose, living their lives trying to save the nation. They did not wince in the face of brutal conflict: "they were swifter than eagles, they were stronger than lions" (verse 23). The daughters of Israel weep—how the mighty have fallen!

David's most personal grief is reserved for Jonathan, his most cherished friend (verse 26). His love for Jonathan was more precious than that of a wife. Yet he lies slain on the mountains—how the mighty have fallen! The song is simultaneously intimate and public. David found the words to match his bitter personal loss and that of the nation. In our contemporary culture—which wants to silence heartfelt speech, cover up our losses, and deny the pain of loss and grief—David's lamentation feels utterly honest and healing.

Yet David's honest grieving is matched by his uninhibited jubilation. After David had conquered Jerusalem and made it the capital city of Israel's united tribes, he brought the ark of the covenant from its temporary location to its new sanctuary in Jerusalem (6:2–4). The sacred ark had guided God's people through the wilderness, led them into the promised land, and embodied the memories and aspirations of the nation. David and all the Israelites danced without restraint before the ark, the most revered symbol of God's presence among them (6:5). The several musical instruments that accompany the singing and dancing—"lyres and harps and tambourines and castanets and cymbals"—represent a range of instruments used in festive occasions. The march accompanying the ark seems to be an occasion somewhere between unreserved celebration and liturgical procession.

Reflection and discussion

• Why is music so effective in helping people grieve their losses?

• What prevents me from expressing the full range of sorrow and joy in my worship of God?

• How do music, dancing, and procession help me give honor to God?

Prayer

Lord of the ancient covenant, your servant David was free to express the full range of his emotions, from heartfelt grief to exuberant joy. Fill me with awe in your presence and lift up my heart so that I may worship you without reserve.

SUGGESTIONS FOR GROUP SESSION 2

1. If there are newcomers who were not present for the first group session, introduce them now.

2. You may want to pray this prayer as a group:
   Holy God, source of life and salvation for your people, you bring down the arrogant and mighty while lifting up the humble and lowly. As refuge and protector of your people, be our steady source of confidence in our trials and lift up our hearts to worship you without reserve. Help us be compassionate when others experience failure and rejoice when others achieve success. Teach us to trust in you in all circumstances of our lives, freeing us to express the full range of emotions, from heartfelt grief to exuberant joy.

3. Ask one or more of the following questions:
   - What was your biggest challenge in Bible study over this past week?
   - What did you learn about yourself this week?

4. Discuss lessons 1 through 6 together. Assuming that group members have read the Scripture and commentary during the week, there is no need to read it aloud. As you review each lesson, you might want to briefly summarize the Scripture passages of each lesson and ask the group what stands out most clearly from the commentary.

5. Choose one or more of the questions for reflection and discussion from each lesson to talk over as a group. You may want to ask group members which question was most challenging or helpful to them as you review each lesson.

6. Keep the discussion moving, but don't rush the discussion in order to complete more questions. Allow time for the questions that provoke the most discussion.

7. Instruct group members to complete lessons 7 through 12 on their own during the six days before the next group meeting. They should write out their own answers to the questions as preparation for next week's group discussion.

8. Conclude by praying aloud together the prayer at the end of lesson 6, or any other prayer you choose.

David commanded the chiefs of the Levites to appoint their kindred as the singers to play on musical instruments, on harps and lyres and cymbals, to raise loud sounds of joy. 1 CHRONICLES 15:16

Orchestra and Chorus for the Sanctuary

1 CHRONICLES 15:14–28 *¹⁴So the priests and the Levites sanctified themselves to bring up the ark of the Lord, the God of Israel. ¹⁵And the Levites carried the ark of God on their shoulders with the poles, as Moses had commanded according to the word of the Lord.*

¹⁶David also commanded the chiefs of the Levites to appoint their kindred as the singers to play on musical instruments, on harps and lyres and cymbals, to raise loud sounds of joy. ¹⁷So the Levites appointed Heman son of Joel; and of his kindred Asaph son of Berechiah; and of the sons of Merari, their kindred, Ethan son of Kushaiah; ¹⁸and with them their kindred of the second order, Zechariah, Jaaziel, Shemiramoth, Jehiel, Unni, Eliab, Benaiah, Maaseiah, Mattithiah, Eliphelehu, and Mikneiah, and the gatekeepers Obed-edom and Jeiel. ¹⁹The singers Heman, Asaph, and Ethan were to sound bronze cymbals; ²⁰Zechariah, Aziel, Shemiramoth, Jehiel, Unni, Eliab, Maaseiah, and Benaiah were to play harps according to Alamoth; ²¹but Mattithiah, Eliphelehu, Mikneiah, Obed-edom, Jeiel, and Azaziah were to lead with lyres according to the Sheminith. ²²Chenaniah, leader of the Levites in music, was to direct the music, for he understood it. ²³Berechiah and Elkanah were to be gatekeepers for the ark. ²⁴Shebaniah, Joshaphat, Nethanel, Amasai, Zechariah, Benaiah, and Eliezer, the priests, were to blow the trumpets before the ark of God. Obed-edom and Jehiah also were to be gatekeepers for the ark.

^{25}So David and the elders of Israel, and the commanders of the thousands, went to bring up the ark of the covenant of the Lord from the house of Obed-edom with rejoicing. ^{26}And because God helped the Levites who were carrying the ark of the covenant of the Lord, they sacrificed seven bulls and seven rams. ^{27}David was clothed with a robe of fine linen, as also were all the Levites who were carrying the ark, and the singers, and Chenaniah the leader of the music of the singers; and David wore a linen ephod. ^{28}So all Israel brought up the ark of the covenant of the Lord with shouting, to the sound of the horn, trumpets, and cymbals, and made loud music on harps and lyres.

The transfer of the ark of the covenant to its tabernacle in Jerusalem is carefully and elaborately narrated by the chronicler. Determined to handle the movement of the sacred ark in accordance with the prescripts of the Torah, David ordered that only the Levites were to carry it.

According to the prescriptions of Moses, the ark was fitted with rings and poles so that it could be carried by hand, rather than on a cart. So, after being properly sanctified, "the Levites carried the ark of God on their shoulders with the poles, as Moses had commanded according to the word of the Lord" (verses 14–15).

After completing the arrangements for properly carrying the ark of the covenant, David turned his attention to organizing the playing and singing to accompany the ark. The fact that the transfer of the ark was accompanied by music is mentioned also in the parallel text of 2 Samuel 6, but in Chronicles there is much more detail and the task is entrusted only to musicians from among the Levites. David delegated the musical appointments to "the chiefs of the Levites," who then appoint "the singers to play on musical instruments, on harps and lyres and cymbals, to raise loud sounds of joy" (verse 16).

The appointed heads of the singers are Heman, Asaph, and Ethan (verse 17). Following these are listed the singers of "the second order" (verse 18). Each of these is assigned to groups based on their musical specialty: Heman, Asaph, and Ethan would sound the bronze cymbals, while the others are divided between the harps and the lyres (verses 19–21). This choir and ensemble is led by Chenaniah who would serve as conductor (verse 22). The musical ensemble is completed with six priests assigned "to blow the trumpets" (verse 24). In addition, the gatekeepers for the ark are named, although their role in bringing the ark to the sanctuary is uncertain. Now, with all the assignments given, the procession with the ark of the covenant may begin.

David was accompanied by the elders of Israel and the commanders of the thousands in the joyful pageant (verse 25). Seven bulls and seven rams were offered in sacrifice because God helped the Levites in their perilous work of carrying the ark (verse 26). A ceremonial white robe made of fine linen was worn by all those associated with the transfer of the ark: David, the Levites carrying the ark, the musicians in the procession, and the leader of music (verse 27). In addition, David wore a linen ephod, a distinctly priestly garment. The horns, trumpets, cymbals, harps, and lyres accompanied the singing and joyful shouting that accompanied the liturgical procession to Jerusalem.

Before David, music was not organized for the purpose of corporate worship. But David saw the value of having a large class of professional musicians for the sacred rituals of the nation. The group of musicians assigned to the procession with the ark continued to serve in the music ministry of the sanctuary. Chronicles records that out of the 38,000 Levites during David's reign, 4,000 were appointed as musicians "to offer praises to the Lord" (1 Chron 23:5).

Reflection and discussion

- What would be the advantage of having a national choir and orchestra for the sacred rituals of Israel?

- What role do liturgical vestments play in processions and sacred ceremonies?

- What does the fact that Israel's most sacred symbol, the ark of the covenant, is made for carrying in procession indicate about the religion of God's people?

- What religious processions do I hold in my memory? What was the role of music in these rituals?

Prayer

King of glory, I lift up my voice and sing praises to you. As you led your people through the wilderness and into the land you promised, now lead me to your holy dwelling where I may praise you with the joyful song of my heart.

Sing to the Lord, all the earth. Tell of his salvation from day to day. Declare his glory among the nations, his marvelous works among all the peoples. 1 CHRONICLES 16:23–24

Singing Praises before the Ark of the Covenant

1 CHRONICLES 16:7–13, 23–36 *⁷Then on that day David first appointed the singing of praises to the Lord by Asaph and his kindred.*

⁸O give thanks to the Lord, call on his name,
make known his deeds among the peoples.
⁹Sing to him, sing praises to him,
tell of all his wonderful works.
¹⁰Glory in his holy name;
let the hearts of those who seek the Lord rejoice.
¹¹Seek the Lord and his strength,
seek his presence continually.
¹²Remember the wonderful works he has done,
his miracles, and the judgments he uttered,
¹³O offspring of his servant Israel,
children of Jacob, his chosen ones.

²³Sing to the Lord, all the earth.
Tell of his salvation from day to day.
²⁴Declare his glory among the nations,
his marvelous works among all the peoples.

²⁵*For great is the Lord, and greatly to be praised;*
   he is to be revered above all gods.
²⁶*For all the gods of the peoples are idols,*
   but the Lord made the heavens.
²⁷*Honor and majesty are before him;*
   strength and joy are in his place.
²⁸*Ascribe to the Lord, O families of the peoples,*
   ascribe to the Lord glory and strength.
²⁹*Ascribe to the Lord the glory due his name;*
   bring an offering, and come before him.
Worship the Lord in holy splendor;
   ³⁰*tremble before him, all the earth.*
   The world is firmly established; it shall never be moved.
³¹*Let the heavens be glad, and let the earth rejoice,*
   and let them say among the nations, "The Lord is king!"
³²*Let the sea roar, and all that fills it;*
   let the field exult, and everything in it.
³³*Then shall the trees of the forest sing for joy*
   before the Lord, for he comes to judge the earth.
³⁴*O give thanks to the Lord, for he is good;*
   for his steadfast love endures forever.
³⁵*Say also:*
   "Save us, O God of our salvation,
      and gather and rescue us from among the nations,
   that we may give thanks to your holy name,
      and glory in your praise.
³⁶*Blessed be the Lord, the God of Israel,*
   from everlasting to everlasting."
Then all the people said "Amen!" and praised the Lord.

When the procession had ended and the ark of the covenant had reached the tabernacle, David offered sacrifices to the Lord and taught the people this song of thanksgiving. Asaph and his kindred led the hymn, which is a compilation of verses from three psalms adapted for the occasion: Psalms 105, 96, and 106. The use of the psalms in this context witnesses to the ways the songs of Israel express fitting prayer in every period of its history, whether it be the setting of this scene at the beginning of Israel's monarchy, the postexilic setting in which Chronicles was written, or in our own times.

The hymn begins with an extensive invitation to give praise to the Lord, comprised of the opening verses of Psalm 105. The number of imperatives is remarkable: give thanks, make known, sing, tell, glory, rejoice, seek, and remember. Part of giving thanks to God is making known to the surrounding peoples who the Lord is and what he has done (verse 8). The ways of making God known are singing his praises, telling others his wonderful works, glorifying his name, and living with a joyful heart (verses 9–10). Although Israel throughout its history was continually tempted to look to other religious, political, and military resources, they must be a people who look to the Lord for all their needs, who "seek his presence continually" (verse 11). They must call to mind God's actions—his wonderful works, his miracles, and the judgments he uttered—and they must remember their own identity as the offspring of Jacob/Israel and as God's "chosen ones" (verse 12–13).

The hymn of praise continues with a reworked version of Psalm 96, adapting it for the narrative setting of the ark's transfer to Jerusalem. In the opening exhortation, "Sing to the Lord, all the earth," it will become clear that all the earth embraces both the earth's nations and peoples as well as the natural world (verses 23–24). Again, a key way of giving praise and thanks to God is by narrating who God is and what he has done: sing to the Lord, tell of his salvation, and declare his glory. God's desire for salvation is universal, so the praise of God encompasses all time, all places, and all peoples.

The following verses offer reasons for singing praise to God, for undeniably he is great and worthy of praise (verse 25). God is revered "above all gods," both those idols fabricated by other nations and whatever people trust in, strive for, and worship (verse 26). For indeed, the Lord's worthiness lies in what he had made and what he has done, whereas these worthless gods have no existence. The Lord is deserving of "honor and majesty," while "strength and joy" reside where the ark of the covenant rests (verse 27).

All the "families of the peoples" are invited to come to the tabernacle of the Lord's presence in Jerusalem, to worship God and to bring an offering to the assembly (verses 28–29). God's reign is demonstrated in both the natural world and the human sphere; the order and stability evident in the natural world demonstrate the reliability of the Lord's reign in the human sphere as well (verse 30). So the heavens and the earth may rejoice, and the peoples of all the nations may acclaim, "The Lord is king!" (verse 31).

All nature—the roaring sea, the exulting field, and the singing forest—rejoices in the Lord. Yet they express gladness not just for God's creative presence, but because God is coming "to judge the earth" (verses 32–33). God's judgment restores order and harmony to the earth. When human injustice brings destruction, God's justice sets things right. The social order and the order of creation are inevitably intertwined. So it is proper that nature and humanity should rejoice together in the great refrain: "O give thanks to the Lord, for he is good; for his steadfast love endures forever" (verse 34).

The final verses, adapted from a few lines of Psalm 106, express the proper stance for God's people in prayer: offering humble petition for God's continual help and deliverance (verse 35). This prayer may be offered by the community gathered with David at the tabernacle, the chronicler's community after the exile, and by people in every age. The song of praise ended as all the people responded, "Amen!" and praised the Lord.

Reflection and discussion

- For what religious event might this song be appropriately sung today?

- How does music and song help God's people to "remember the wonderful works he has done"?

- What indicates that Israel's praise of God is universal in its scope and expanse?

- What are some ways, according to this song of praise, for making God known to the people around us?

- In what ways do human justice and injustice have consequences for the sea, field, and forest?

Prayer

Lord of all, I sing for joy with the heavens and the earth, the roaring sea, the exulting fields, and the trees of the forest. May all creation worship you and may your steadfast love endure forever.

When the burnt offering began, the song to the Lord began also, and the trumpets, accompanied by the instruments of King David of Israel. 2 CHRONICLES 29:27

Temple Sacrifice Accompanied by Instruments and Song

2 CHRONICLES 5:11–14 ¹¹*Now when the priests came out of the holy place (for all the priests who were present had sanctified themselves, without regard to their divisions), ¹²and all the levitical singers, Asaph, Heman, and Jeduthun, their sons and kindred, arrayed in fine linen, with cymbals, harps, and lyres, stood east of the altar with one hundred twenty priests who were trumpeters, ¹³it was the duty of the trumpeters and singers to make themselves heard in unison in praise and thanksgiving to the Lord, and when the song was raised, with trumpets and cymbals and other musical instruments, in praise to the Lord,*

"For he is good,
for his steadfast love endures forever,"

the house, the house of the Lord, was filled with a cloud, ¹⁴so that the priests could not stand to minister because of the cloud; for the glory of the Lord filled the house of God.

2 CHRONICLES 29:25–30 ²⁵*[The king] stationed the Levites in the house of the Lord with cymbals, harps, and lyres, according to the commandment of David and of Gad the king's seer and of the prophet Nathan, for the commandment was from the Lord through his prophets. ²⁶The Levites stood with the instruments of*

David, and the priests with the trumpets. [27]*Then Hezekiah commanded that the burnt offering be offered on the altar. When the burnt offering began, the song to the Lord began also, and the trumpets, accompanied by the instruments of King David of Israel.* [28]*The whole assembly worshiped, the singers sang, and the trumpeters sounded; all this continued until the burnt offering was finished.* [29]*When the offering was finished, the king and all who were present with him bowed down and worshiped.* [30]*King Hezekiah and the officials commanded the Levites to sing praises to the Lord with the words of David and of the seer Asaph. They sang praises with gladness, and they bowed down and worshiped.*

The musical tradition begun by David when he transferred the ark of the covenant to Jerusalem was continued and expanded during the reign of Solomon, when he brought the ark into the holy of holies in the newly constructed temple. When the ark was set in its place, the priests exited the temple and were joined east of the altar by the temple choir and orchestra, all wearing robes of fine linen (verses 11–12). This impressive musical performance consisted of a large numbers of Levites, again led by Asaph, Heman, Jeduthun, and their sons and kindred, singing and playing cymbals, harps, and lyres. If we assume the list of the temple musicians given in 1 Chronicles 25 as historically accurate, the total number was 288. These were joined by 120 twenty priests sounding trumpets.

The music was sung by the liturgical ensemble and presumably by all the people. The antiphon, found in several places throughout the psalms, praises God's goodness and constancy in the language of the covenant with Moses: "for he is good, for his steadfast love endures forever" (verse 13). We may imagine a cantor and choir singing antiphonally, as in Psalm 136, reminding the nation of God's covenant loyalty and worshipping God with grateful acceptance.

Praise for the Lord's goodness and constancy was expressed most solemnly by worshiping in Jerusalem's temple. God's steadfast love was sacramentally experienced in this ancient liturgy of song and sacrifices, established by David and preserved by his descendants. As the song of praise and thanksgiving was raised, the temple was filled with a cloud, "for the glory of the Lord filled the house of God" (verse 14). This tangible reminder of God's presence with the Israelites in the tabernacle during their wilderness travel may have been expressed by smoking incense in the days of the chronicler.

This musical tradition of the temple continued into the reign of King Hezekiah, about three centuries after David. In his reform efforts, Hezekiah sought to return the nation and its temple to the glory of the united monarchy. For the temple's rededication, the king assembled the Levites, who stood with "cymbals, harps, and lyres" ("the instruments of David"), while the priests stood with the trumpets (verses 25–26). When Hezekiah ordered the sacrifice be offered on the altar, the assembly prostrated themselves in worship, the singers sang with their instruments, and the trumpeters sounded. All of this continued until the offering was consumed (verses 27–28).

After the sacrifice had been offered, the king and his entourage also bowed down and prostrated themselves. The Levites then sing hymns created by David and Asaph, both of whom are named as composers of collections of songs in the Book of Psalms. The singers praised God with "gladness," with festive merriment, and they too bowed and worshiped the Lord.

Reflection and discussion

- What type of music is the greatest help for me in my worship of God?

- In what new ways do these scenes help me to imagine the sacrificial worship of God's people?

- The kind of divine love expressed in the musical refrain (verse 13) emphasizes God's constancy, faithfulness, and steadfastness. What does this say about the quality of God's love for me and about what God expects of me?

- What are the various elements of the temple service (verses 27–28)? Why is each part important for the fullness of worship?

- Why is music and song so integral to the worship of God presented in the Bible?

Prayer

O give thanks to the Lord, for he is good, for his steadfast love endures forever. I worship you, O God! With songs of praise and with gladness in my heart, I bow down in adoration in your presence.

Begin a song to my God with tambourines, sing to my Lord with cymbals. Raise to him a new psalm; exalt him, and call upon his name. JUDITH 16:1

Judith's Hymn of Praise

JUDITH 15:12—16:16 *¹²All the women of Israel gathered to see her, and blessed her, and some of them performed a dance in her honor. She took ivy-wreathed wands in her hands and distributed them to the women who were with her; ¹³and she and those who were with her crowned themselves with olive wreaths. She went before all the people in the dance, leading all the women, while all the men of Israel followed, bearing their arms and wearing garlands and singing hymns.*

¹⁴Judith began this thanksgiving before all Israel, and all the people loudly sang this song of praise.

16 *¹And Judith said,*
> *Begin a song to my God with tambourines,*
> > *sing to my Lord with cymbals.*
> *Raise to him a new psalm;*
> > *exalt him, and call upon his name.*
> *²For the Lord is a God who crushes wars;*
> > *he sets up his camp among his people;*
> > *he delivered me from the hands of my pursuers.*
> *³The Assyrian came down from the mountains of the north;*
> > *he came with myriads of his warriors;*
> *their numbers blocked up the wadis,*
> > *and their cavalry covered the hills.*

⁴He boasted that he would burn up my territory,
    and kill my young men with the sword,
and dash my infants to the ground,
    and seize my children as booty,
    and take my virgins as spoil.
⁵But the Lord Almighty has foiled them
    by the hand of a woman.
⁶For their mighty one did not fall by the hands of the young men,
    nor did the sons of the Titans strike him down,
    nor did tall giants set upon him;
but Judith daughter of Merari
    with the beauty of her countenance undid him.
⁷For she put away her widow's clothing
    to exalt the oppressed in Israel.
She anointed her face with perfume;
    ⁸she fastened her hair with a tiara
    and put on a linen gown to beguile him.
⁹Her sandal ravished his eyes,
    her beauty captivated his mind,
    and the sword severed his neck!
¹⁰The Persians trembled at her boldness,
    the Medes were daunted at her daring.
¹¹Then my oppressed people shouted;
    my weak people cried out, and the enemy trembled;
    they lifted up their voices, and the enemy were turned back.
¹²Sons of slave-girls pierced them through
    and wounded them like the children of fugitives;
    they perished before the army of my Lord.
¹³I will sing to my God a new song:
O Lord, you are great and glorious,
    wonderful in strength, invincible.
¹⁴Let all your creatures serve you,
    for you spoke, and they were made.
You sent forth your spirit, and it formed them;
    there is none that can resist your voice.

^{15}For the mountains shall be shaken to their foundations with the waters;
   before your glance the rocks shall melt like wax.
But to those who fear you
   you show mercy.
^{16}For every sacrifice as a fragrant offering is a small thing,
   and the fat of all whole burnt offerings to you is a very little thing;
but whoever fears the Lord is great forever.

This canticle is ascribed to Judith, a heroine who became the pride of all the women of Israel because she became an instrument of God's liberating power at a dark time in the life of the people. The women of Israel sing, play percussion instruments, and dance to celebrate the victory, a tradition that began with Miriam, who led all the women in celebrating God's deliverance from the Egyptians at the sea (Exod 15). Here, Judith leads the festivity, adorning the women with wreaths of ivy and olive, and leading them in a triumphant dance. The men follow, bearing their weapons, wearing garlands, and singing hymns. As Judith begins this hymn of praise, all the people sing along at full volume.

Judith invites the assembly to acclaim God, singing with tambourines and cymbals while calling on God's name (verse 1). The hymn honors the Lord, the one "who crushes wars" (verse 2). The victory was a work of God who intervened in a totally amazing way to rescue Israel from an impending and total defeat. The peril faced by Israel is described in striking terms: the Assyrian general invading with massive numbers of warriors, filling the valleys and covering the hills (verse 3). His arrogance is highlighted with sarcasm, as he boasts of how he will devastate and humiliate the people of Israel (verse 4).

The description of Israel's rescue is equally dramatic. For the mighty Lord has thwarted the enemy "by the hand of a woman," a great humiliation (verse 5). The disgrace of the enemy is further magnified by naming possible foes of great strength. Their mighty general, Holofernes, did not fall at the hands of young men, nor was he struck down by the sons of Titans or tall giants, but Judith overcame him with her beauty (verse 6). She prepared for battle not by accumulating weapons of war, but by embellishing her loveliness. The extended description of her attractiveness captivates the minds of the singers, just as it had mesmerized Holofernes, until the shocking decisive moment: "Her sandal ravished his eyes, her beauty captivated his mind, and the sword severed his neck!" (verse 9).

The story of Judith's courageous deed is narrated in the previous chapters: how, like Jael in the time of Deborah (Judg 4), she made her way unarmed into the tent of the enemy's general, and how, like David after his defeat of Goliath (1 Sam 17), she severed her opponent's head with his own sword. Making her way back to the Israelite camp, she instructed the troops to hang the severed head of Holofernes on the ramparts and then to attack the enemy. When the enemy troops saw the head and realize they were without a leader, they fled in terror as the Israelites pursued and overtook them (verses 11–12). As the account teaches, God works through the lowly and the humble to defeat the strong and the proud.

Judith returns to her song of praise, lifting her voice to God, who is "great and glorious" (verse 13). God is the one who created everything as he spoke, filling creatures with his divine spirit (verse 14). In God's presence, mountains shudder and rocks melt, but for those who fear the Lord, he shows mercy (verse 15). Awe and reverence of God is greater than any sacrifice and the way to live forever in his compassionate goodness (verse 16).

Judith is an archetype for the Jewish tradition to emphasize God's preference for what is simple and meek, but for that reason chosen to manifest divine power. She shows the calling and mission of women, called to be men's equal and to play a significant role in the plan of God for the world. No wonder she is given the highest praise by her own people: "You are the glory of Jerusalem, you are the great boast of Israel, you are the great pride of our nation!" (15:9).

Reflection and discussion

- Why would the Israelites choose to remember the account of Judith in song?

- Why is fear of the Lord so much better and life-giving than sacrifices and burnt offerings?

- What makes Judith an exemplary figure whose story is told in generation after generation?

Prayer

O God, our help in ages past and our hope for years to come, I sing to you a new song, you who are great, glorious, strong, and invincible. Give me a fearful reverence for your presence and a joyful trust in your unfathomable ways.

Sing praises to the Lord with the lyre, with the lyre and the sound of melody. With trumpets and the sound of the horn make a joyful noise before the King, the Lord. PSALM 98:5–6

Praising God with Musical Instruments, Song, and Dance

PSALM 98:1–9

¹*O sing to the Lord a new song,*
    for he has done marvelous things.
His right hand and his holy arm
    have gotten him victory.
²*The Lord has made known his victory;*
    he has revealed his vindication in the sight of the nations.
³*He has remembered his steadfast love and faithfulness*
    to the house of Israel.
All the ends of the earth have seen
    the victory of our God.
⁴*Make a joyful noise to the Lord, all the earth;*
    break forth into joyous song and sing praises.
⁵*Sing praises to the Lord with the lyre,*
    with the lyre and the sound of melody.
⁶*With trumpets and the sound of the horn*
    make a joyful noise before the King, the Lord.

⁷*Let the sea roar, and all that fills it;*
   the world and those who live in it.
⁸*Let the floods clap their hands;*
   let the hills sing together for joy
⁹*at the presence of the Lord, for he is coming*
   to judge the earth.
He will judge the world with righteousness,
   and the peoples with equity.

PSALM 150:1–6

¹*Praise the Lord!*
Praise God in his sanctuary;
   praise him in his mighty firmament!
²*Praise him for his mighty deeds;*
   praise him according to his surpassing greatness!
³*Praise him with trumpet sound;*
   praise him with lute and harp!
⁴*Praise him with tambourine and dance;*
   praise him with strings and pipe!
⁵*Praise him with clanging cymbals;*
   praise him with loud clashing cymbals!
⁶*Let everything that breathes praise the Lord!*
   Praise the Lord!

Psalm 98 begins with a call for the Israelites to "sing to the Lord a new song." The reason for this invitation is the "marvelous things" God has done and the "victory" he has won through his great power (98:1). There is no indication what particular events the original composer might have had in mind, so in the worship of Israel, the marvelous things and victory express a summary of all the Lord's saving deeds throughout their history. Yet these victories were not only for Israel's sake; rather, they were revealed "in the sight of the nations." Whether it be Israel's liberation from Egypt, the conquest of the land, the rescue from Assyria, or the deliverance from Babylon, these are divine manifestations "all the ends of the earth have seen" (98:2–3).

The next call to praise the Lord is an extended invitation addressed to the whole world. "All the earth" is invited to "make a joyful noise," to "break forth into joyous song," and to "sing praises to the Lord" (98:4). Praises are sung to the accompaniment of the "lyre," which creates the "melody" of the songs. The "trumpet" is a straight metal instrument and the "horn" is the natural horn of an animal, particularly a goat or a ram. These create a joyful noise, but not a melody.

The psalm finally turns to the entire creation to join in the praise (98:7–9). This cosmic assembly of the sea, the world, rivers, and hills roar, clap their hands, and sing together for joy. The universe is united in one purpose: to exalt the divine King, who is "coming to judge the earth." The great hope of creation is that God will "judge the world with righteousness, and the peoples with equity," so that the Lord will reestablish the original harmony of creation and bring about a kingdom of justice and peace.

The God of Israel is the God of all the nations and the God of all creation. Although God has been committed to the Israelites from the beginning, blessing Israel is not the extent of God's purposes. The blessings of Abraham, which have gone out to all the nations in Christ's church, affect the whole world. In this ecology of praise, the entire creation, in countless visible and audible ways, echoes humanity's enthusiasm for the marvelous things God has done.

Psalm 150 sets a seal on the Book of Psalms, the hymnbook of the people of God. It is a hymn of pure praise; the imperative, "Praise the Lord!" rings in every line. Its few verses detail the where, why, how, and who of this praise of God.

The "where," the location of God's praise, is described as "his sanctuary," the holy shrine or temple where he dwells on earth, and "his mighty firmament," the dome in the heavens above which his throne is established (150:1). Worshipers on earth and in heaven are invited to join their praise to God. The "why" of praise is described as God's "mighty deeds" and his "surpassing greatness," nothing more specific than this. Actually, everything that the previous 149 psalms have affirmed about God offers the reasons and the content for this praise.

The "how" of praise seems to incorporate every known musical instrument that human genius has invented (150:3–5). The trumpets were played by priests, the lute, harp, and cymbals were played by Levites, and the tambourine, strings, and pipe were played by anyone. Both music within the temple liturgy and music played in festive celebrations were forms of praise to God. And, finally, the "who" of praise includes "everything that breathes," all living creatures (150:6). The community that praises God includes not just Israelite, not just human, and not just earthly. All creation—visible and invisible, earthly and heavenly, timely and eternal—adores God with unencumbered praise.

Reflection and discussion

- Do I prefer stringed, wind, or percussion instruments to praise God?

- Are some instruments best for liturgical worship and others for festive praise, or does it matter?

- Do I ever sing to God during my personal time of prayer? What could songs add to my conversing with God?

Prayer

King of the universe, whether I fall on my knees in worship or clap my hands in praise, I honor you for your mighty deeds and your surpassing greatness. I join with all the creatures of the earth, sky, and sea to give you praise.

Your cheeks are comely with ornaments, your neck with strings of jewels. We will make you ornaments of gold, studded with silver. SONG 1:10–11

The Song of King Solomon

SONG OF SOLOMON 1:1–17 *The Song of Songs, which is Solomon's.*

²Let him kiss me with the kisses of his mouth!
For your love is better than wine,
  ³your anointing oils are fragrant,
your name is perfume poured out;
  therefore the maidens love you.
⁴Draw me after you, let us make haste.
  The king has brought me into his chambers.
We will exult and rejoice in you;
  we will extol your love more than wine;
  rightly do they love you.
⁵I am black and beautiful,
  O daughters of Jerusalem,
like the tents of Kedar,
  like the curtains of Solomon.
⁶Do not gaze at me because I am dark,
  because the sun has gazed on me.
My mother's sons were angry with me;
  they made me keeper of the vineyards,
  but my own vineyard I have not kept!
⁷Tell me, you whom my soul loves,
  where you pasture your flock,

where you make it lie down at noon;
for why should I be like one who is veiled
  beside the flocks of your companions?
[8]*If you do not know,*
  O fairest among women,
follow the tracks of the flock,
  and pasture your kids
  beside the shepherds' tents.
[9]*I compare you, my love,*
  to a mare among Pharaoh's chariots.
[10]*Your cheeks are comely with ornaments,*
  your neck with strings of jewels.
[11]*We will make you ornaments of gold,*
  studded with silver.
[12]*While the king was on his couch,*
  my nard gave forth its fragrance.
[13]*My beloved is to me a bag of myrrh*
  that lies between my breasts.
[14]*My beloved is to me a cluster of henna blossoms*
  in the vineyards of En-gedi.
[15]*Ah, you are beautiful, my love;*
  ah, you are beautiful;
  your eyes are doves.
[16]*Ah, you are beautiful, my beloved,*
  truly lovely.
Our couch is green;
  [17]*the beams of our house are cedar,*
  our rafters are pine.

The Song of Songs is a collection of love poetry celebrating the joys and longings of love. It is attributed to King Solomon, but this is more like a dedication than an assertion of authorship. Like love songs through the ages, it is rich in poetic beauty and metaphor, expressing love's yearning, admiration, playfulness, seeking, and finding. The singers are primarily the man, who appears as both a shepherd and a king, and the woman. There appear also the daughters of Jerusalem, who serve as a kind of chorus.

The canticle begins as the woman expresses her yearning for the kisses of her beloved. She speaks to him and about him in the same breath. It is uncertain whether the man is physically near or present only in her imaginative musings. The imagery appeals to multiple senses: kisses to the touch, wine to the taste, and fragrant oils and perfume to the smell (verses 2–3). The woman envisions the man drawing her into his chambers, and the maidens who accompany her rejoice and delight in him. She understands why they adore him too (verse 4). The urgency of the voices, the lack of clarity, the rush of images, and the combination of attraction and confusion— this ambiguity expresses the new and disconcerting emotions in the young lovers.

The woman then addresses the daughters of Jerusalem, telling them that she is dark and attractive: dark like the tents made from the hair of black goats and beautiful like the curtains of Solomon's temple (verse 5). The daughters of Jerusalem gaze on her exotic loveliness, which the sun has darkened as she was forced by her brothers to work in the vineyards (verse 6).

The woman then teasingly begins a dialogue with her beloved, asking where she can meet him for a midday rendezvous as he rests his flock. She suggests that she may lurk around the flocks of his companions if he does not direct her to his own (verse 7). The man playfully responds that she should follow the tracks of the flock and pasture her own beside the tents of the other shepherd (verse 8). Praising her strength and attractiveness, he then compares her to a mare among the stallions of Pharaoh's chariots (verse 9). Like the heads and necks of the royal horses, she is bedecked with adornments, which he promises to enhance with gold and silver jewelry (verses 10–11).

The woman then returns to describing fragrant scents. The sweet fragrance of her spikenard drifts through the air as he rests on his couch. The charm and intimacy of his presence is like the scents of myrrh and blossoms of henna (verses 12–14). Exchanging tributes, he exclaims that she is beautiful, with soft eyes like doves, and she responds by declaring his attractiveness and calling him "beloved." And finally, she describes their house and furniture as made of sweet-smelling wood, perhaps a true home or maybe an outdoor dwelling among the trees (verses 15–17).

The two lovers are single-minded in their devotion to each other and to their relationship. They admire the physical charms of one another and speak freely about their desire to be together. The Song can be read as an extended commentary on God's description of creation as "very good," especially in reference to the creation of man and woman. In these verdant scenes, the tangled estrangement between men and women seems unknotted. They exist in a fresh, new creation, in which male-female sexuality is neither exploitative nor hierarchic.

Reflection and discussion

- How does the Song of Songs exemplify the common themes of love poetry?

- How does this lyric poetry involve all the senses?

- How do people in love remedy the insecurities of each other?

Prayer

Divine Beloved, you have planted within me a deep desire for you and a longing for your presence. Help me to seek and find you, and enable me to trust you with all my heart.

SUGGESTIONS FOR FACILITATORS, GROUP SESSION 3

1. Welcome group members and ask if there are any announcements anyone would like to make.

2. You may want to pray this prayer as a group:
   Lord of all creation, whether we fall on our knees in worship or clap our hands in praise, we honor you for your mighty deeds and your surpassing greatness. Give us a fearful reverence for your presence and a joyful trust in your unfathomable ways. We sing to you, who are great, glorious, strong, and invincible, and we join with all the creatures of the earth, sky, and sea to give you praise. Give us always a deep desire for you and a longing for your presence as you lead us to your holy dwelling.

3. Ask one or more of the following questions:
   - Which message of Scripture this week speaks most powerfully to you?
   - What is the most important lesson you learned through your study this week?

4. Discuss lessons 7 through 12. Choose one or more of the questions for reflection and discussion from each lesson to discuss as a group. You may want to ask group members which question was most challenging or helpful to them as you review each lesson.

5. Remember that there are no definitive answers for these discussion questions. The insights of group members will add to the understanding of all. None of these questions require an expert.

6. After talking about each lesson, instruct group members to complete lessons 13 through 18 on their own during the six days before the next group meeting. They should write out their own answers to the questions as preparation for next week's group discussion.

7. Ask the group if anyone is having any particular problems with the Bible study during the week. You may want to share advice and encouragement within the group.

8. Conclude by praying aloud together the prayer at the end of one of the lessons discussed. You may add to the prayer based on the sharing that has occurred in the group.

What more was there to do for my vineyard that I have not done in it? When I expected it to yield grapes, why did it yield wild grapes? ISAIAH 5:4

Isaiah's Song of the Vineyard

ISAIAH 5:1–7

¹Let me sing for my beloved
   my love-song concerning his vineyard:
My beloved had a vineyard
   on a very fertile hill.
²He dug it and cleared it of stones,
   and planted it with choice vines;
he built a watchtower in the midst of it,
   and hewed out a wine vat in it;
he expected it to yield grapes,
   but it yielded wild grapes.
³And now, inhabitants of Jerusalem
   and people of Judah,
judge between me
   and my vineyard.
⁴What more was there to do for my vineyard
   that I have not done in it?
When I expected it to yield grapes,
   why did it yield wild grapes?
⁵And now I will tell you
   what I will do to my vineyard.

I will remove its hedge,
  and it shall be devoured;
I will break down its wall,
  and it shall be trampled down.
⁶I will make it a waste;
  it shall not be pruned or hoed,
  and it shall be overgrown with briers and thorns;
I will also command the clouds
  that they rain no rain upon it.
⁷For the vineyard of the Lord of hosts
  is the house of Israel,
and the people of Judah
  are his pleasant planting;
he expected justice,
  but saw bloodshed;
righteousness,
  but heard a cry!

From among the many picturesque illustrations and metaphors of the prophet Isaiah comes this Song of the Vineyard. It presents us with the prophet chanting a "love-song" on behalf of his "beloved," whom we soon realize is God, a song about the love of God for his vineyard (verse 1). He tells of the great care his beloved applied in cultivating the vineyard, clearing the stones from the hillside and turning them into a stable watchtower and wall to keep the animals out (verse 2). After planting it with the best variety of vines, he constructed a winepress with vats for pressing the juice from the grapes and for settling the juice to make wine. But, tragically, when it came time to harvest the grapes, instead of being plump and sweet, they were sour and wild. Rather than a chant of joyful praise, it becomes a song about disappointment.

The owner of the vineyard speaks directly to the listeners, asking advice because he needs to make a decision about the vineyard's future: "What more was there to do for my vineyard that I have not done in it? (verse 4). Sadly, the implied answer is "nothing." The owner decides to stop cultivating the vineyard, removing his care and protection (verses 5–6). By removing its hedge and breaking down its wall, he will open the vineyard to wild animals that will eat the grapes and damage the vines. Because they are not pruned, the vines will grow too long to support the fruit, and because the ground is not hoed, the weeds will grow and compete for the vine's nutrients and moisture. The owner will even command the clouds not to water the vineyard with vital rains.

All becomes clear in the final verse. The song is about the relationship between God and his people (verse 7). They, the listeners, are the vineyard about to be destroyed. For the owner is the Lord of hosts. The divine judgment on Israel and Judah is the absence of God's sustaining presence, leaving the people and its land prey to those who will take advantage of its weakness. Israel and Judah have not met God's expectations. They were to be beneficial fruit, a blessing to the nations. They were expected to maintain a society whose values were shaped by justice and righteousness. God's people will be abandoned to those who would overrun and conquer them.

Yet Isaiah is a prophet of both realism and hope. He speaks harsh words of judgment, and he offers compassionate words of promise for the future. Although God's judgments are punitive, they are also remedial. For the prophet who chanted the destruction of the vineyard also offers this song of praise: "I will give thanks to you, O Lord, for though you were angry with me, your anger turned away, and you comforted me. Surely God is my salvation; I will trust, and will not be afraid, for the Lord God is my strength and my might; he has become my salvation" (Isa 12:1–2).

Reflection and discussion

- Why do love songs often end in tragic disappointment? Why do the grief and longing continue?

- What project have I attempted that might be similar to the owner's cultivation of the vineyard? What were the results?

- What is the purpose of God asking the people to judge for themselves what he should do with the vineyard?

- Jesus took the images of Israel's Song of the Vineyard to compose his parable of the vineyard (Matt 21:33–44). What does this add to your understanding of God's plan for the vineyard?

Prayer

God of the vineyard, you have planted, protected, nourished, and cultivated your people. Yet we have neglected your grace and failed to bear the fruit you desire. Forgive me, merciful Lord, and help me trust in your salvation.

Get you up to a high mountain, O Zion,
herald of good tidings; lift up your voice with strength,
O Jerusalem, herald of good tidings, lift it up, do not fear;
say to the cities of Judah, "Here is your God!" ISAIAH 40:9

Proclaiming God's Comfort and Glad Tidings

ISAIAH 40:1–11

¹*Comfort, O comfort my people,*
* says your God.*
²*Speak tenderly to Jerusalem,*
* and cry to her*
that she has served her term,
* that her penalty is paid,*
that she has received from the Lord's hand
* double for all her sins.*
³*A voice cries out:*
"In the wilderness prepare the way of the Lord,
* make straight in the desert a highway for our God.*
⁴*Every valley shall be lifted up,*
* and every mountain and hill be made low;*
the uneven ground shall become level,
* and the rough places a plain.*
⁵*Then the glory of the Lord shall be revealed,*
* and all people shall see it together,*
* for the mouth of the Lord has spoken."*

⁶*A voice says, "Cry out!"*
   And I said, "What shall I cry?"
All people are grass,
   their constancy is like the flower of the field.
⁷*The grass withers, the flower fades,*
   when the breath of the Lord blows upon it;
   surely the people are grass.
⁸*The grass withers, the flower fades;*
   but the word of our God will stand forever.
⁹*Get you up to a high mountain,*
   O Zion, herald of good tidings;
lift up your voice with strength,
   O Jerusalem, herald of good tidings,
   lift it up, do not fear;
say to the cities of Judah,
   "Here is your God!"
¹⁰*See, the Lord God comes with might,*
   and his arm rules for him;
his reward is with him,
   and his recompense before him.
¹¹*He will feed his flock like a shepherd;*
   he will gather the lambs in his arms,
and carry them in his bosom,
   and gently lead the mother sheep.

The second part of the Book of Isaiah, which is pure prophetic poetry without any historical narrative, was chanted from exile by the one often called the Prophet of Consolation. The Babylonians had destroyed Jerusalem, the temple was in ruins, the priesthood was scattered, the dynasty of David was finished, and Judah's most influential citizens were in exile. Those who witnessed the devastation in Jerusalem sang the sorrowful canticles of Lamentations with their continual refrain, "There is none to comfort her" (Lam 1:2, 9, 16–17, 21). Jerusalem was like a woman who has lost her husband and children, sitting in desolation.

But now the time of sorrow is over and the voice of God declares, "Comfort, O comfort my people" (verse 1). These joyful lyrics look beyond the captivity of God's people in Babylon, expressing the hope of a restored nation. Although the fall of Jerusalem was an act of divine judgment on an unfaithful city, the prophet expresses certainty that Jerusalem's astonishing restoration is imminent. Although finding language adequate to describe the ways of God is difficult in every age, the words of the prophet are something far beyond normal human condolences. With tender language, God is comforting, pardoning, and redeeming Jerusalem. Her prison sentence is ended, her sin has been paid for, and she need fear nothing more from God's hand (verse 2).

For God comes out of the wilderness for his repentant people (verse 3). The triumphal procession of the divine King is the Lord's gracious reentry into the life of the outcast nation. Nothing can deter him, neither deserts, nor mountains, nor valleys (verse 4). A supernaturally shaped highway will speed his coming to the people. Then "the glory of the Lord," God's wonderful manifestation, will be accomplished and seen by "all people" (verse 5). The whole world will realize God saving purpose with a certainly derived from the fact that it has been revealed from the very mouth of God.

In contrast to the unstoppable coming of the King of all people, humanity is powerless. "All people are grass," quickly grown and quickly withered (verses 6–7). They are like the wildflowers, whose colors brighten the field in springtime but soon fade to brown when the hot winds blow upon them. All the great powers of the world are fleeting, no more to be feared than grass and flowers. The divine Spirit that breaths out destruction over all human pride is the same Spirit that has inspired the word of God. "The grass withers, the flower fades; but the word of our God will stand forever" (verse 8). Whatever lies ahead for God's people, they may know that God's promises will not fail them.

The message of God's salvation is not for Jerusalem alone; it is for the whole world. This evangelization begins as Jerusalem becomes a "herald of good tidings," a proclaimer of good news to all the cities of Judah around her (verse 9). The essence of the message is, "Here is your God!" The coming of God to the world was the good news then, as it still is today. The Lord God is both a divine warrior (verse 10) and a compassionate shepherd (verse 11). The divine "arm," raised in triumph, is lowered to hold his people like lambs. These two complementary aspects of God's nature are welcome news for his people in every age.

Reflection and discussion

• How is this living prophecy a comfort to me as I hear it today?

• What does it mean for me to "prepare the way of the Lord"?

• In what ways do I experience God as both a divine warrior and a gentle shepherd?

Prayer

Come, Good Shepherd of your flock, rescue the captives and give comfort to those who feel far away. As we experience the fleeting nature of our earthly lives, let us know that the word of your promises remains forever.

For a long time I have held my peace, I have kept still and restrained myself; now I will cry out like a woman in labor, I will gasp and pant. ISAIAH 42:14

Isaiah's Hymn of Praise

ISAIAH 42:10–16

¹⁰*Sing to the Lord a new song,*
  his praise from the end of the earth!
Let the sea roar and all that fills it,
  the coastlands and their inhabitants.
¹¹*Let the desert and its towns lift up their voice,*
  the villages that Kedar inhabits;
let the inhabitants of Sela sing for joy,
  let them shout from the tops of the mountains.
¹²*Let them give glory to the Lord,*
  and declare his praise in the coastlands.
¹³*The Lord goes forth like a soldier,*
  like a warrior he stirs up his fury;
he cries out, he shouts aloud,
  he shows himself mighty against his foes.
¹⁴*For a long time I have held my peace,*
  I have kept still and restrained myself;
now I will cry out like a woman in labor,
  I will gasp and pant.
¹⁵*I will lay waste mountains and hills,*
  and dry up all their herbage;

I will turn the rivers into islands,
   and dry up the pools.
[16]*I will lead the blind*
   by a road they do not know,
by paths they have not known
   I will guide them.
I will turn the darkness before them into light,
   the rough places into level ground.
These are the things I will do,
   and I will not forsake them.

The entire earth with all its inhabitants is enjoined to become an immense choir to acclaim the Lord with exaltation and to give him glory. People everywhere are invited to join in this hymn of praise, whether they be on the farthest seas or on the highest mountains (verses 10–12). God is making salvation known to all the earth. The instruction to "sing to the Lord a new song" corresponds to the new work that God is about to do. The imminent return of God's people from exile heralds a divine deliverance whose ultimate implications are worldwide. The God who has shown himself faithful to Israel in their captivity will be faithful in bringing redemption to the whole world. Even distant places like Kedar, representing the dwellers of the Arabian desert, and Sela, an Edomite city that many have identified with Petra, are urged to sing and discover their ultimate purpose by joining God's people in the most blessed of all acts—giving glory and praise to the Lord.

The pressing reason for singing a song of praise is that God, who may often appear to be silent and inactive, is about to burst forth on behalf of his people (verses 13–14). While in exile, the people of Jerusalem felt like God had abandoned them, but now he goes forth "like a warrior." This is one of Israel's most ancient images for God, as in the Song of the Sea and the Song of Deborah. After all, the origins of Israel were associated with battles that God fought and won: the victory at the sea over the Egyptian armies, the victories during the time of Joshua and the judges over the Canaanites, and the victories over the Philistines during the time of David. The divine warrior "stirs up his fury," thinking about the wrongs the enemy has done to his people, and them lets out a great shout, both to fortify himself and to frighten his foes.

When the song changes to the first person, God himself speaks and the image is changed from the divine warrior to the "woman in labor." The common factor in both images is the outcry at the climactic moment. All the apparent quiet and inactivity, whether in silently preparing for battle or in the nine months of pregnancy, comes to an end in the cry of attack or of birth pangs. So it is with God, says Isaiah's song of praise. The Lord, who has long been silent, will be so no more.

God's vehement words combine judgment and salvation (verses 15–16). God's judgment on evil is presented with images of destruction, dryness, and drought, but its goal is freedom and fruitfulness. The Lord brings forth a new world of salvation, delivering the blind from darkness. So with us, unless God acts on our behalf, we are utterly blind and helpless. We may feel that nothing is happening, that God is silent and has forgotten about us. But if we wait patiently, God will save us and not forsake us. We must learn to trust and discern the signs of divine action even when they seem to be hidden and quiet.

Reflection and discussion

- How do I experience God "like a warrior"? How does this enrich my understanding of God?

- How do I experience God "like a woman in labor"? How does this enrich my understanding of God?

- When have I felt that God is silent and has forgotten about me?

- What words and images in this song help me to trust in God?

- When have I discovered that waiting patiently on the Lord was a necessary preparation for God's saving action?

Prayer

Holy Lord, who is like both a fierce warrior and a woman giving birth, help me to trust in you, especially during those times when you seem to be silent and far away from me. Give me a deep faith in you, even in the quiet darkness.

As soon as all the peoples heard the sound of the horn, pipe, lyre, trigon, harp, drum, and entire musical ensemble, all the peoples, nations, and languages fell down and worshiped the golden statue that King Nebuchadnezzar had set up. DANIEL 3:7

Nebuchadnezzar's Orchestra in Babylon

DANIEL 3:3–18 *³So the satraps, the prefects, and the governors, the counselors, the treasurers, the justices, the magistrates, and all the officials of the provinces, assembled for the dedication of the statue that King Nebuchadnezzar had set up. When they were standing before the statue that Nebuchadnezzar had set up, ⁴the herald proclaimed aloud, "You are commanded, O peoples, nations, and languages, ⁵that when you hear the sound of the horn, pipe, lyre, trigon, harp, drum, and entire musical ensemble, you are to fall down and worship the golden statue that King Nebuchadnezzar has set up. ⁶Whoever does not fall down and worship shall immediately be thrown into a furnace of blazing fire." ⁷Therefore, as soon as all the peoples heard the sound of the horn, pipe, lyre, trigon, harp, drum, and entire musical ensemble, all the peoples, nations, and languages fell down and worshiped the golden statue that King Nebuchadnezzar had set up.*

⁸Accordingly, at this time certain Chaldeans came forward and denounced the Jews. ⁹They said to King Nebuchadnezzar, "O king, live forever! ¹⁰You, O king, have made a decree, that everyone who hears the sound of the horn, pipe, lyre, trigon, harp, drum, and entire musical ensemble, shall fall down and worship the golden statue, ¹¹and whoever does not fall down and worship shall be thrown into a furnace of blazing fire. ¹²There are certain Jews whom you have appointed over the affairs of the province of Babylon: Shadrach, Meshach, and Abednego. These pay no heed to you, O King. They do not serve your gods and they do not worship the golden statue that you have set up."

¹³Then Nebuchadnezzar in furious rage commanded that Shadrach, Meshach, and Abednego be brought in; so they brought those men before the king. ¹⁴Nebuchadnezzar said to them, "Is it true, O Shadrach, Meshach, and Abednego, that you do not serve my gods and you do not worship the golden statue that I have set up? ¹⁵Now if you are ready when you hear the sound of the horn, pipe, lyre, trigon, harp, drum, and entire musical ensemble to fall down and worship the statue that I have made, well and good. But if you do not worship, you shall immediately be thrown into a furnace of blazing fire, and who is the god that will deliver you out of my hands?"

¹⁶Shadrach, Meshach, and Abednego answered the king, "O Nebuchadnezzar, we have no need to present a defense to you in this matter. ¹⁷If our God whom we serve is able to deliver us from the furnace of blazing fire and out of your hand, O king, let him deliver us. ¹⁸But if not, be it known to you, O king, that we will not serve your gods and we will not worship the golden statue that you have set up."

The story of King Nebuchadnezzar of Babylon and his golden statue is told by the Jewish narrator as a humorous satire. Beginning with the list of government officials with their pompous titles—satraps, the prefects, and the governors, the counselors, the treasurers, the justices, the magistrates, and all the officials of the provinces—the storyteller mocks the haughtiness of the royal court (verse 3). The towering statue accentuates the king's grandiose view of his empire and its wealth. These elements serve to entertain the readers while also communicating an inspiring message of hope.

Nebuchadnezzar's supremacy is ridiculed with expressions of his absolute and universal power. All "peoples, nations, and languages" are commanded to "fall down and worship," an order that is awkwardly repeated eight times, creating a rigid and stilted narrative. The penalty for not obeying the command, "a furnace of blazing fire," is also repeatedly recorded (verses 6, 11, 15, 17). Its highly exaggerated heat expresses the insecurity of the king's tyrannical power that must be backed up with the threat of absolute punishment.

The list of musical instruments, often called the "orchestra of Nebuchadnezzar," includes six different instruments—the horn, pipe, lyre, trigon, harp, drum—each of which produces a unique sound that is blended with other instruments to create the "entire musical ensemble." (verses 5, 7, 10, 15). Although the beauty of music is ideally designed to renew and transform the human spirit, it is used here to manipulate the assembly, to get them to conform to the will of a tyrannical ruler. Consider the ways marching music was employed at Nazi assemblies or at Communist May Day ceremonies to parade the newest military weapons. Evil imprisons creation's beauty and uses it as a sinister tool for control. This music of idolatry symbolizes all manipulative forces that try to get people to bow down.

Each time the orchestra plays, all the assembled peoples must fall prostrate in homage: "As soon as all the peoples heard the sound of the horn, pipe, lyre, trigon, harp, drum, and entire musical ensemble, all the peoples, nations, and languages fell down and worshiped the golden statue" (verse 7). The lists of officials, instruments, and peoples repetitively emphasize the robotic subservience of the assembly to the king's will. Every aspect of the ceremony is taken to an extreme, revealing a ruler who has lost all sense of proportion and perspective.

A discordant note sounds when the king's advisors inform the king about the three obstinate Jews (verse 8). The satire continues as they repeat the king's command, as if he needs reminding (verses 9–11). The three Jews are introduced using their Babylonian names—Shadrach, Meshach, and Abednego—which are continually repeated for comedic effect. They are the fly in the ointment of Nebuchadnezzar's big moment: paying no heed to the king's command, rejecting his gods, and refusing to worship his golden statue (verse 12). The news enrages the king and, once more, he repeats his monotonous command, ending with his sarcastic question: Who is the god that will deliver you out of my hands?" (verse 15).

In contrast to the repetitive, long-windedness of the previous part of the narrative, the response of the three Jews is confident and frank (verses 16–18). They are clear about what they must do. They know that God's glory is of greater value than their own lives, and they have chosen to revere God, not knowing whether they will honor him with the witness of their deliverance from the flames or the witness of their martyrdom.

Reflection and discussion

- What indicates to me that the Jewish narrator is telling this tale with tongue in the cheek and a smile on the face?

- What is the difference between using music to worship God and using it to manipulate people into idolatry?

- How can a person stand firm and be a contrarian in the face of tyrannical authority?

Prayer

O Lord, God of our ancestors, you alone are worthy of all glory and praise. Give us the grace to be faithful to your will as we have come to know it, and guard our hearts from falling prey to the snares of idolatry.

They walked around in the midst of the flames, singing hymns to God and blessing the Lord. Then Azariah stood still in the fire and prayed aloud. DANIEL 3:24–25

Chanting Prayer in the Flaming Furnace

DANIEL 3:24–29, 34–41 ²⁴*They walked around in the midst of the flames, singing hymns to God and blessing the Lord.* ²⁵*Then Azariah stood still in the fire and prayed aloud:*

²⁶*"Blessed are you, O Lord, God of our ancestors, and worthy of praise;*
    and glorious is your name forever!
²⁷*For you are just in all you have done;*
    all your works are true and your ways right,
    and all your judgments are true.
²⁸*You have executed true judgments in all you have brought upon us*
    and upon Jerusalem, the holy city of our ancestors;
    by a true judgment you have brought all this upon us because of our sins.
²⁹*For we have sinned and broken your law in turning away from you;*
    in all matters we have sinned grievously.

³⁴*For your name's sake do not give us up forever,*
    and do not annul your covenant.
³⁵*Do not withdraw your mercy from us,*
for the sake of Abraham your beloved
    and for the sake of your servant Isaac
    and Israel your holy one,

^{36}*to whom you promised*
  to multiply their descendants like the stars of heaven
  and like the sand on the shore of the sea.
^{37}*For we, O Lord, have become fewer than any other nation,*
  and are brought low this day in all the world because of our sins.
^{38}*In our day we have no ruler, or prophet, or leader,*
  no burnt offering, or sacrifice, or oblation, or incense,
  no place to make an offering before you and to find mercy.
^{39}*Yet with a contrite heart and a humble spirit may we be accepted,*
  ^{40}*as though it were with burnt offerings of rams and bulls,*
  or with tens of thousands of fat lambs;
  such may our sacrifice be in your sight today,
  and may we unreservedly follow you,
  for no shame will come to those who trust in you.
^{41}*And now with all our heart we follow you;*
  we fear you and seek your presence.

After narrating the rage of Nebuchadnezzar at the three Jews who refused to worship his golden statue, the storyteller states that the obstinate men were cast into the furnace of blazing fire. At this point, the Greek version of Daniel has inserted hymns sung in the midst of the flames. The first is sung by Azariah (the Hebrew name for Abednego) as he "stood still in the fire and prayed aloud," like a martyr who is ready to suffer death in order not to betray his conscience and his faith (verse 25).

Azariah's song lifts up the voice of God's people experiencing the harsh trial of exile and persecution. It begins with a typical Jewish benediction: "Blessed are you, O Lord, God of our ancestors, and worthy of praise; and glorious is your name forever!" (verse 26). The song then proceeds to declare that God is just and right in the suffering that has come upon Israel, a punishment with which God purifies his sinful people (verses 27–29). We hear a penitential prayer that gives way not to despair but to confident hope.

In the present tragedy, the song seeks hope from the past, in the covenant promises God made to Israel's ancestors, to Abraham, Isaac, and Jacob/ Israel (verses 34–36). To them God pledged countless descendants, land, and blessings. So, even if justice demands that God's people be punished for their sins, they may be certain that God's mercy and pardon will have the last word. This is a season of humiliation for Israel, left without king, prophet, priests, temple, or sacrifices, a time of the Lord's seeming absence (verses 37–38).

Chanting in the name of all God's people, the singer offers God the most acceptable and precious sacrifice of all: "a contrite heart and a humble spirit" (verse 39). The singer has dedicated the people's trials and sufferings to God, praying that God might accept the offering as a sign of conversion and re-dedication to the covenant. Through this inner renewal, the shame of the past is overcome, and a new spirit of trust is gained (verses 40–41). With confidence in a better future, he promises to follow the Lord, fear his name, and seek his presence.

Reflection and discussion

- What can I do to renew my life and restore my hope after a time of sin and shame?

- In what ways has the church experienced a time of humiliation like the trials of ancient Israel? Why is "a contrite heart and a humble spirit" the most acceptable offering we can make to God?

Prayer

Lord our God, for your name's sake do not give us up forever, do not annul your covenant, and do not withdraw your mercy from us. Offering up our trials to you, we ask you to forgive our sins and help us trust in your mercy.

Bless the Lord, spirits and souls of the righteous; sing praise to him and highly exalt him forever. Bless the Lord, you who are holy and humble in heart; sing praise to him and highly exalt him forever. DANIEL 5:86–87

Song of the Three Companions in Babylon

DANIEL 3:51–57, 82–90 ⁵¹*Then the three with one voice praised and glorified and blessed God in the furnace:*

⁵²*"Blessed are you, O Lord, God of our ancestors,*
    and to be praised and highly exalted forever;
And blessed is your glorious, holy name,
    and to be highly praised and highly exalted forever.
⁵³*Blessed are you in the temple of your holy glory,*
    and to be extolled and highly glorified forever.
⁵⁴*Blessed are you who look into the depths from your throne on the cherubim,*
    and to be praised and highly exalted forever.
⁵⁵*Blessed are you on the throne of your kingdom,*
    and to be extolled and highly exalted forever.
⁵⁶*Blessed are you in the firmament of heaven,*
    and to be sung and glorified forever.
⁵⁷*"Bless the Lord, all you works of the Lord;*
    sing praise to him and highly exalt him forever.

⁸²*"Bless the Lord, all people on earth;*
    sing praise to him and highly exalt him forever.
⁸³*Bless the Lord, O Israel;*
    sing praise to him and highly exalt him forever.
⁸⁴*Bless the Lord, you priests of the Lord;*
    sing praise to him and highly exalt him forever.
⁸⁵*Bless the Lord, you servants of the Lord;*
    sing praise to him and highly exalt him forever.
⁸⁶*Bless the Lord, spirits and souls of the righteous;*
    sing praise to him and highly exalt him forever.
⁸⁷*Bless the Lord, you who are holy and humble in heart;*
    sing praise to him and highly exalt him forever.
⁸⁸*"Bless the Lord, Hananiah, Azariah, and Mishael;*
    sing praise to him and highly exalt him forever.
For he has rescued us from Hades and saved us from the power of death,
    and delivered us from the midst of the burning fiery furnace;
    from the midst of the fire he has delivered us.
⁸⁹*Give thanks to the Lord, for he is good,*
    for his mercy endures forever.
⁹⁰*All who worship the Lord, bless the God of gods,*
    sing praise to him and give thanks to him,
    for his mercy endures forever."

As the king's servants continued to stoke the flames, an angel of the Lord went into the flames with the three Jewish companions "and made the inside of the furnace as though a moist wind were whistling through it (verse 50). The pain of the trial disappeared in the face of the companions' confident trust in God. Then the three men, who are here presented with their Hebrew names—Hananiah, Azariah, and Mishael—"praised and glorified and blessed God in the furnace" with this song of praise.

The hymn is sung in antiphonal style. We can imagine the soloist or choir intoning the incantation, "Blessed are you," followed by some aspect of the divine presence. The congregation then continually responds with the chant, "and to be praised and highly exalted forever." Blessings in Scripture work in two directions: God blesses creation with his presence, graces, and goodness; in return, creation lifts up its blessings to God. After receiving so many blessings from God's generosity, the world blesses God by praising, thanking, and exalting him.

This long and beautiful hymn is known in the church's liturgical tradition as *Benedictus es Domine*, "Blessed are you, O Lord." Each invocation rises to God like billowing incense, each curling upward through the air in similar but unique clouds. As litanies demonstrate, prayer does not eschew repetition but uses it to convey the intensity and multiple nuances of the singers' feelings and gratefulness.

The first six invocations are addressed directly to God (verses 52–56). God who is sitting on his throne in the heavens is also close to his people and gazes upon them. The transcendent Lord of the cosmos is also the God who dwells with his people. This divine presence evokes awe and holy fear in the people and, at the same time, helps them feel protected and safe.

The hymn then turns toward creation, calling upon all "works of the Lord" to "sing praise to him and highly exalt him forever" (verse 57). In giving praise to God, creation acquires its full meaning and purpose. It becomes an immense choir with various but harmonized voices, a view of creation fully alive and praising its Creator.

After calling upon all the elements of creation to praise God, the song continues evoking all the people of the earth (verse 82). The scope is then focused on Israel, then the priests, followed by the "servants of the Lord," "spirits and souls of the righteous," and the "holy and humble in heart" (verses 83–87). From among these witnesses to faith, truth, and justice, the three companions emerge: Hananiah, Azariah, and Mishael, who have been saved from the fiery flames and sing this universal hymn.

Like nightmares that evaporate in the rays of the morning sunshine, fears dissolve and suffering is eased when prayer expresses total abandonment to God. The three companions were rescued as they were filled with trust, expectation, and hope. And they can offer no better thanks than to let their voices resound in this litany as they "bless," "praise," and "exalt" the universal Lord.

Reflection and discussion

- Why is praise and adoration the highest form of prayer?

- What attitudes within myself sometimes diminish my natural desire to give glory and thanks to God?

- What is the purpose of such repetitious chanting of the same words in litany form?

Prayer

Blessed are you, O Lord, who has bestowed such generous gifts upon me, I offer you praise and thanksgiving with all my heart. You are worthy to receive a symphony of worship from all your creatures throughout the earth.

SUGGESTIONS FOR FACILITATORS, GROUP SESSION 4

1. Welcome group members and ask if anyone has any questions, announcements, or requests.

2. You may want to pray this prayer as a group:
   God of the vineyard, who has planted, protected, nourished, and cultivated your people, Good Shepherd of your flock, who rescues the captives and give comfort to those who feel far away, and Holy Lord, who is like both a fierce warrior and a woman giving birth, we sing your praises with an imagination filled with your wonders. Give us the grace to be faithful to your will as we have come to know it, and give us confidence that the word of your promises remains forever.

3. Ask one or more of the following questions:
   - What is the most difficult part of this study for you?
   - What insights stand out to you from the lessons this week?

4. Discuss lessons 13 through 18. Choose one or more of the questions for reflection and discussion from each lesson to discuss as a group. You may want to ask group members which question was most challenging or helpful to them as you review each lesson.

5. Keep the discussion moving, but allow time for the questions that provoke the most discussion. Encourage the group members to use "I" language in their responses.

6. After talking over each lesson, instruct group members to complete lessons 19 through 24 on their own during the six days before the next group meeting. They should write out their own answers to the questions as preparation for next week's session.

7. Ask the group what encouragement they need for the coming week. Ask the members to pray for the needs of one another during the week.

8. Conclude by praying aloud together the prayer at the end of one of the lessons discussed. You may choose to conclude the prayer by asking members to pray aloud any requests they may have.

"My soul magnifies the Lord, and my spirit rejoices in God my Savior, for he has looked with favor on the lowliness of his servant. Surely, from now on all generations will call me blessed." LUKE 1:46–48

Mary's Canticle of Praise

LUKE 1:46–55

⁴⁶And Mary said,

"My soul magnifies the Lord,

⁴⁷and my spirit rejoices in God my Savior,

⁴⁸for he has looked with favor on the lowliness of his servant.

Surely, from now on all generations will call me blessed;

⁴⁹for the Mighty One has done great things for me,

and holy is his name.

⁵⁰His mercy is for those who fear him

from generation to generation.

⁵¹He has shown strength with his arm;

he has scattered the proud in the thoughts of their hearts.

⁵²He has brought down the powerful from their thrones,

and lifted up the lowly;

⁵³he has filled the hungry with good things,

and sent the rich away empty.

⁵⁴He has helped his servant Israel,

in remembrance of his mercy,

⁵⁵according to the promise he made to our ancestors,

to Abraham and to his descendants forever."

S ince Mary knew the Old Testament well, she would have been quite familiar with the passages from the Scriptures of Israel that echo throughout her canticle. She is part of a long line of biblical women who sing songs of praise: Miriam (Exod 15:20–21), Deborah (Judg 5), Hannah (1 Sam 2:1–10), and Judith (Jdt 16:1–17). Mary's canticle also resonates with the Psalms, the daily hymns of the Jewish people. She sings back to God the truths that she learned in her daily reflection on the word of God. As Elizabeth's unborn child leapt in her womb and as Elizabeth exclaimed, "Blessed are you among women and blessed is the fruit of your womb," Mary responded in one of the most beloved songs of the Scriptures.

Traditionally called the Magnificat, from its first words in the Latin version, *Magnificat anima mea Dominum*, meaning "My soul magnifies the Lord" (verse 46), Mary's canticle is one of the oldest Christian hymns and perhaps the earliest Marian hymn. In the Byzantine tradition, it is called the Ode of the Theotokos. The lyrics have been set to music by composers of the East and West throughout the centuries.

Mary's song demonstrates that she is the representative of God's people. The mercy shown to her reflects the mercy that God has shown to Israel and is a response to the promises God made long ago. The young Mary yields herself completely to God's will and sings with complete confidence that what had been promised has now come to pass. She is a model of living faith because she recognized what God was doing through her, she accepted it joyfully, and she was humble enough to give God all the glory.

The song speaks of Mary's humility: she was mindful of her status as a humble village maiden whose "lowliness" the Lord has regarded with favor (verse 48). God has unexpectedly reversed her low status so that now she can sing, "all generations will call me blessed." Likewise, God reverses all that people have come to expect: he disperses the arrogant, throws down the rulers, and sends the rich away empty. But God also lifts up the lowly, fills the hungry, and comes to the aid of Israel (verses 51–54). What God has done for Mary models and anticipates what God will do for the poor, oppressed, and powerless of the world.

It is striking that the lines that speak of what God promised through the prophets for the future age to come is proclaimed in the past tense. In this way the song expresses confidence and certainty in God's establishment of justice and mercy. Mary is so sure that God will do what is promised that she proclaims it as an accomplished reality. In Mary's song of the God who raises the lowly and brings down the mighty, who fills the hungry while sending the rich away empty, Luke the evangelist is introducing a theme prominent throughout his gospel and into his Acts of the Apostles. This reversal expected for the time of judgment has already begun, and God's choice of Mary is evidence of it.

Reflection and discussion

- What seem to be some of the primary emotions Mary felt in singing this canticle of praise?

- How does Jesus fulfill the themes of Mary's Canticle throughout his life and into the life of this church?

- How does my life reflect God's concern for justice, mercy, and liberation?

Prayer

Mighty Lord, you have done great things for me and for all your people. Thank you for continuing to fulfill your promises to me, and help me to be grateful for all you have done from generation to generation.

"By the tender mercy of our God, the dawn from on high will break upon us, to give light to those who sit in darkness and in the shadow of death, to guide our feet into the way of peace."

LUKE 1:78–79

Canticle of Zechariah

LUKE 1:67–79 *⁶⁷Then his father Zechariah was filled with the Holy Spirit and spoke this prophecy:*

⁶⁸"Blessed be the Lord God of Israel,
> *for he has looked favorably on his people and redeemed them.*
⁶⁹He has raised up a mighty savior for us
> *in the house of his servant David,*
⁷⁰as he spoke through the mouth of his holy prophets from of old,
> *⁷¹that we would be saved from our enemies and from the hand of all*
> > *who hate us.*
⁷²Thus he has shown the mercy promised to our ancestors,
> *and has remembered his holy covenant,*
⁷³the oath that he swore to our ancestor Abraham,
> *to grant us ⁷⁴that we, being rescued from the hands of our enemies,*
might serve him without fear, ⁷⁵in holiness and righteousness
> *before him all our days.*
⁷⁶And you, child, will be called the prophet of the Most High;
> *for you will go before the Lord to prepare his ways,*
⁷⁷to give knowledge of salvation to his people
> *by the forgiveness of their sins.*
⁷⁸By the tender mercy of our God,
> *the dawn from on high will break upon us,*

93

*⁷⁹to give light to those who sit in darkness and in the shadow of death,
   to guide our feet into the way of peace."*

Immediately after the birth and naming of John, his father, Zechariah, was "filled with the Holy Spirit" and chanted this prophetic canticle. He voices his confidence that God's plan of salvation is moving to its completion with the new divine actions told in the opening chapter of Luke's gospel. The song falls into two parts: first, praise of God for bringing his plan to completion by sending Jesus to the world (verses 68–75); and second, praise of the role of his son, John, as God's prophet, preparing the way for God's saving work (verses 76–79).

Zechariah's canticle is the second of the four hymns in the infancy narrative of Luke's gospel. It is traditionally called the Benedictus, receiving its name from its first word in Latin, *Benedictus Dominus Deus Israel*, meaning "Blessed be the Lord God of Israel" (verse 68). Since the early centuries, the Benedictus has been sung in the morning prayer of the church's liturgy because of its praise for the coming of the Redeemer and its allusion to Christ' coming as the dawn to give light to those in darkness.

Full of allusions to the Old Testament, these verses are distinctly Jewish. In the family of David, the prophets had promised power to God's people to defend themselves against their enemies. While the Jews had impatiently borne the yoke of the Romans, they had continually yearned for their deliverer. Now, God has raised up "a mighty savior" from David's line (verses 69–71). The deliverance was now at hand, the fulfillment of God's covenant with Israel and God's oath to Abraham (verses 72–73). Through the prophetic work of John the Baptist and the coming of the Messiah, the God of Israel is redeeming his people.

But this fulfillment is described as a liberation not for the sake of worldly power but so that God's people "might serve him without fear, in holiness and righteousness before him all our days" (verses 74–75). Rescued from their enemies and liberated to worship God, the nation is experiencing a new exodus. They are now free to serve in responsiveness to God's will, a worship that spans the lifetimes of God's faithful ones.

The second part of the canticle is an address by Zechariah to his own son, who would play an essential role in God's saving plan. He will be God's prophet, teaching an understanding of salvation and preaching the remission of sins (verses 76–77). The prophecy that John "will go before the Lord to prepare his ways" is an allusion to the words of Isaiah 40:3, by which Luke describes the mission of John the Baptist (Luke 3:4). As Luke develops the figure of John, he associates this forerunner with the message of salvation, the forgiveness of sins, and the baptism of repentance.

In contrast to John, the role of the Messiah, as "the dawn" that comes from God, is to scatter the darkness of sin and death and guide God's people "into the way of peace" (verses 78–79). The Messiah's light refers to his coming to humanity, his teaching God's ways, and his ministering salvation. All of these messianic works are the concrete expressions of God's compassion, his "tender mercy." As the rising sun, Jesus brings salvation by showing God's people "the way" that leads to a complete and harmonious relationship with God. Instruction in this "way" of Jesus is the mission of the remainder of Luke's writing.

Reflection and discussion

• How does Zechariah's canticle compare and contrast to Mary's canticle?

• In what ways does the canticle of Zechariah describe the redemption God brings to his people as a new "exodus"?

- How does the song express God's unfolding plan from Abraham to the coming of the Messiah?

- Why did Zechariah's canticle become the morning prayer of Christ's church?

- Who helped "prepare the way" for God's unfolding his plan of salvation in my life?

Prayer

Lord God of Israel, you brought redemption to your chosen people after a long time of waiting. Help me to be faithful to your new covenant, to live as your child in freedom, and to worship you in holiness all my days.

And suddenly there was with the angel a multitude of the heavenly host, praising God and saying, "Glory to God in the highest heaven, and on earth peace among those whom he favors!" LUKE 2:13–14

The Angels Sing Glory to God

LUKE 2:8–14 ⁸*In that region there were shepherds living in the fields, keeping watch over their flock by night. ⁹Then an angel of the Lord stood before them, and the glory of the Lord shone around them, and they were terrified. ¹⁰But the angel said to them, "Do not be afraid; for see—I am bringing you good news of great joy for all the people: ¹¹to you is born this day in the city of David a Savior, who is the Messiah, the Lord. ¹²This will be a sign for you: you will find a child wrapped in bands of cloth and lying in a manger." ¹³And suddenly there was with the angel a multitude of the heavenly host, praising God and saying,*

¹⁴"Glory to God in the highest heaven,
*   and on earth peace among those whom he favors!"*

Music has often been called the speech of angels. This avowal couldn't be truer than with the words of a host of angels when Jesus the Messiah was born. The song of the angels is Luke's third hymn of his infancy narrative. It is called the Gloria from the first word of the Latin text: *Gloria in excelsis Deo*, meaning "Glory to God in the highest heaven" (verse 14). Other verses were added very early, forming a hymn that is sung in the eucharistic liturgy after the Kyrie on Sundays outside of Lent and Advent.

The song of the angels is in two parts: "Glory" is offered to God in heaven; "peace" is given to people on earth. Three word pairs show the relationship between the two parts: glory and peace, heaven and earth, and God and "those whom he favors." First, God is glorified for who he is and for what he has done. The heavens rejoice and praise God for the manifestation of salvation, the unfolding of redemptive history culminating in the birth of Jesus. Second, peace is extended to those upon whom God has extended his grace. This peace has vertical implications in that the people to whom God draws near through Jesus will now experience peace with God, and it has horizontal implications in that we are now at peace with one another. The people who welcome the coming of Jesus Christ are the focus of heaven and earth.

The song of the angels is sung only after a single angel has proclaimed the news of the Savior's birth to the shepherds. The message of the angel contains several truths. First, the announcement of Christ's birth is "good news" (verse 10). Second, this good news causes "great joy." The greatest joy in the world is the gospel, the news that God delights to send his Son to be the Savior of the world. Third, this fact impacts "all the people." This is good news not only for the shepherds, but a message of hope and peace for the world.

The fourth truth, the reason the message is good news of great joy, is that "this day" is born "a Savior, who is the Messiah, the Lord," titles of Jesus that will be developed throughout Luke's writings (verse 11). "Savior" points to his role as the one who delivers God's people. "Messiah" designates his regal office as the promised Anointed One from David's family. "Lord" indicates his sovereign authority. Although Jesus is born under the reign of Caesar Augustus, whose titles are just as majestic, the pivotal historical figure is not the Roman emperor but the child Jesus, the royal Savior and Lord of all.

Finally, the truths the angel communicated to the shepherds are authenticated with a sign: "a child wrapped in bands of cloth and lying in a manger" (verse 12). The sign is nothing majestic or triumphant—just a baby wrapped in the cloths of the newborn and lying in a feeding trough for animals. Fortified by these truths, then, and with the full assurance of angels and prophets, we can join with the heavenly host in singing, "Glory to God in the highest heaven, and on earth peace among those whom he favors!"

Reflection and discussion

- Why did God choose to announce the birth of Jesus Christ to shepherds as he was laid in a manger?

- What might the shepherds have been most excited about telling other people?

- God's angel appeared to Zechariah, Mary, and the shepherds during the course of their everyday lives. What does this mean for my own life?

Prayer

God in the highest heaven, bring joy and peace to your people on earth. Help me to be receptive like the shepherds to your revelation and open to accept whatever message you want me to hear.

Guided by the Spirit, Simeon came into the temple; and when the parents brought in the child Jesus, to do for him what was customary under the law, Simeon took him in his arms and praised God. LUKE 2:27-28

Simeon's Canticle in the Temple

LUKE 2:25–32 *²⁵Now there was a man in Jerusalem whose name was Simeon; this man was righteous and devout, looking forward to the consolation of Israel, and the Holy Spirit rested on him. ²⁶It had been revealed to him by the Holy Spirit that he would not see death before he had seen the Lord's Messiah. ²⁷Guided by the Spirit, Simeon came into the temple; and when the parents brought in the child Jesus, to do for him what was customary under the law, ²⁸Simeon took him in his arms and praised God, saying,*

> *²⁹"Master, now you are dismissing your servant in peace,*
> *according to your word;*
> *³⁰for my eyes have seen your salvation,*
> *³¹which you have prepared in the presence of all peoples,*
> *³²a light for revelation to the Gentiles*
> *and for glory to your people Israel."*

The final hymn in Luke's infancy narrative is set in Jerusalem's temple, as Mary and Joseph brought Jesus to the sanctuary for the required dedication of the firstborn son to God. There they were met by Simeon, who had been promised by the Holy Spirit that he would see the

Messiah before his death (verse 26). He represents ancient Israel awaiting its Messiah with expectancy and hope. Now, taking the six-week-old child Jesus in his arms, this devout old man praises God for keeping his word (verses 27–28). The people of ancient Israel can now rest in peace as the new age of God's salvation begins.

The Song of Simeon, like that of Mary and Zechariah, weaves his personal experience of God with what God is doing for all his people. Traditionally called the Nunc dimittis, from the opening words of the Latin, *Nunc dimittis servum tuum*, meaning "Now you are dismissing your servant" (verse 29). For centuries it has been the gospel canticle for the church's night prayer, just as the Benedictus and Magnificat are the canticles of morning prayer and evening prayer respectively. And as with these other gospel canticles, many composers through the ages have set the text to music.

Although brief, the canticle abounds in Old Testament allusions. "For my eyes have seen your salvation" (verse 30) alludes to Isaiah 52:10, proclaiming that "all the ends of the earth shall see the salvation of our God." In the birth of Jesus, the world's salvation has become visible and tangible. The next verse, "which you have prepared in the presence of all peoples" (verse 31), accords with Psalm 98:2, which announces that the Lord "has revealed his vindication in the sight of the nations." Throughout Israel's history, God has been preparing for the world's salvation until the time of fulfillment, which Simeon now recognizes. God intends to extend the salvation that comes in Jesus to all people. Each nation will see what God has done in his Messiah and all will share in its benefits.

Jesus is light, both for the Gentiles and for Israel: "a light for revelation to the Gentiles and for glory to your people Israel" (verse 32). Jesus is the light of salvation to everyone on earth, resulting in revelation to the Gentiles and glory for the people of Israel. The salvation found in Jesus illuminates all people into God's way. The rest of Luke's gospel and Acts reveal that Gentiles participate as equals with Israel in God's salvation, seen and touched in the tiny child resting in the arms of holy Simeon.

Reflection and discussion

- Why was encountering the child Jesus in the temple such a meaningful occasion for Simeon?

- What does Simeon have to teach me about the spiritual value found in waiting?

- How has Christ brought "light" to my life?

Prayer

Lord and Master, you ask me to wait with patience and hope as your will is gradually unfolded. Give me a deep longing for your salvation, and help me trust that you are always faithful to the word of your promises.

And the Word became flesh and lived among us,
and we have seen his glory, the glory as of a
father's only son, full of grace and truth. JOHN 1:14

Hymn to the Divine Word

JOHN 1:1–18 ¹*In the beginning was the Word, and the Word was with God, and the Word was God.* ²*He was in the beginning with God.* ³*All things came into being through him, and without him not one thing came into being. What has come into being* ⁴*in him was life, and the life was the light of all people.* ⁵*The light shines in the darkness, and the darkness did not overcome it.*

⁶*There was a man sent from God, whose name was John.* ⁷*He came as a witness to testify to the light, so that all might believe through him.* ⁸*He himself was not the light, but he came to testify to the light.* ⁹*The true light, which enlightens everyone, was coming into the world.*

¹⁰*He was in the world, and the world came into being through him; yet the world did not know him.* ¹¹*He came to what was his own, and his own people did not accept him.* ¹²*But to all who received him, who believed in his name, he gave power to become children of God,* ¹³*who were born, not of blood or of the will of the flesh or of the will of man, but of God.*

¹⁴*And the Word became flesh and lived among us, and we have seen his glory, the glory as of a father's only son, full of grace and truth.* ¹⁵(*John testified to him and cried out, "This was he of whom I said, 'He who comes after me ranks ahead of me because he was before me.'"*) ¹⁶*From his fullness we have all received, grace upon grace.* ¹⁷*The law indeed was given through Moses; grace and truth came through Jesus Christ.* ¹⁸*No one has ever seen God. It is God the only Son, who is close to the Father's heart, who has made him known.*

The prologue of John's gospel was most probably based on an early Christian hymn to the divine Logos (Word). It links the gospel of Jesus Christ to the whole history of salvation from before creation to the Incarnation. As a hymn, it inserts the gospel into the heritage of ancient Israel and gives it a cosmic context. It convinces the listener that the coming of Christ is not just a historical event but is rooted in the life-creating and light-giving nature of God. The style of the hymn expresses the splendor and significance of its subject, the Word of God manifested to the world.

The phrase "in the beginning" echoes the opening of the Bible in Genesis 1:1. It carries us back before creation to the realm of timeless eternity. "The Word" conveys the idea of God's self-expression. A human word is, in a sense, the extension of a person into his environment; the divine Word is God reaching out, seeking to share his divine being, extending eternal love. Since the Word existed in the beginning, one might think that either "the Word was with God" or "the Word was God." The hymn affirms both (verses 1–2). There is a distinction between the Word and God, but not a separation.

The next stanza speaks of the Word involved in creation (verses 3–4). Because everything came into being through the Word, God first came to be known through creation. Then the Word was manifested to the world as light penetrating the darkness, "the true light that enlightens everyone" (verses 5, 9). The gospel writer seems to have inserted within the original hymn a few verses concerning the role of John the Baptist (verses 6–9, 15). After introducing the Word as the world's light, the evangelist notes that John was not the light, as perhaps many believed, but "he came to testify to the light." These inserted verses honor John by showing his important role in the redemptive history but also making a clear distinction between the Baptist and the Word.

The next stanza voices the rejection of the Word in Israel's history (verses 10–11). Although the unseen Word was at work in the world, the Word remained unrecognized. When the Word was at work within the Torah and prophets of Israel, "his own people did not accept him." The next stanza speaks of those who did accept the revealing Word within the history of Israel (verses 12–13). These were given "power to become children of God," born not through human experience or initiative but generated by God.

The climactic stanza proclaims the incarnation of the Word—"the Word became flesh and lived among us"—the fullest experience of the Word by humanity in the life-giving work of God throughout human history (verse 14). Literally, he pitched his tent, taking up residence among his people in a way far more intimate than when God dwelt in the tabernacle of the wilderness or in the temple of Jerusalem. Although no one has ever seen God, "we have seen his glory," a manifestation of God's presence in a way we can understand.

The final stanza expresses the church's reception of grace through Jesus Christ (verses 16–17). He is the fullness and perfection of all the "grace and truth" God gave to Israel in the past, and "from his fullness we have all received, grace upon grace." Though grace has been given by God through Moses and the law, "grace upon grace," the ultimate grace—an everlasting and rapid succession of blessings—is given through Jesus Christ.

Reflection and discussion

- Why does the evangelist open the gospel "in the beginning" rather than at the conception or birth of Jesus?

- What are the consequences of "receiving" the Word? In what ways have I experienced "grace upon grace" through my relationship with Jesus Christ, the Word made flesh?

Prayer

Word of God, you shine in the world and bring us grace and truth. Cast out the darkness of ignorance, manifest your divine love, and open my heart to the grace upon grace that I experience through the growth of my faith in you.

About midnight Paul and Silas were praying and singing hymns to God, and the prisoners were listening to them. ACTS 16:25

Paul and Silas Sing Hymns in Prison

ACTS 16:23–34 ²³*After they had given them a severe flogging, they threw them into prison and ordered the jailer to keep them securely.* ²⁴*Following these instructions, he put them in the innermost cell and fastened their feet in the stocks.*

²⁵*About midnight Paul and Silas were praying and singing hymns to God, and the prisoners were listening to them.* ²⁶*Suddenly there was an earthquake, so violent that the foundations of the prison were shaken; and immediately all the doors were opened and everyone's chains were unfastened.* ²⁷*When the jailer woke up and saw the prison doors wide open, he drew his sword and was about to kill himself, since he supposed that the prisoners had escaped.* ²⁸*But Paul shouted in a loud voice, "Do not harm yourself, for we are all here."* ²⁹*The jailer called for lights, and rushing in, he fell down trembling before Paul and Silas.* ³⁰*Then he brought them outside and said, "Sirs, what must I do to be saved?"* ³¹*They answered, "Believe on the Lord Jesus, and you will be saved, you and your household."* ³²*They spoke the word of the Lord to him and to all who were in his house.* ³³*At the same hour of the night he took them and washed their wounds; then he and his entire family were baptized without delay.* ³⁴*He brought them up into the house and set food before them; and he and his entire household rejoiced that he had become a believer in God.*

The Scriptures teach in various ways that the gospel of Jesus Christ cannot be held captive. Although Paul and Silas were severely beaten and lashed, imprisoned in the dark innermost cell, with their feet securely shackled, their minds and hearts were free to give praise to God. In the middle of the night, these prisoners were "praying and singing hymns to God" from their cells (verse 25). Although they were in the least comfortable and most solitary place imaginable, they were together in the name of Jesus and, therefore, he was in their presence. Christian faith makes possible an inner freedom that will not be restrained by the bars and chains of a jail.

This is the first recorded imprisonment of Paul, the first of many others by Paul and his companions. Although this was probably their first experience of a jail, they did not yield to despairing thoughts, but they enlivened their solitary hours by raising their thoughts to God, no doubt finding appropriate expression in the Psalms and other biblical hymns they undoubtedly knew by hearts. The Psalms of Israel express every imaginable emotion, leading the singers from lament to trust, from sorrow to praise. Lifting their spirits to God in chanted prayer and heartfelt song enabled them to momentarily forget the pains of their lacerated bodies and tortured limbs with an experience of inner joy. Perhaps they recalled around midnight the words of the Book of Job, which says that God's oppressed people cry out, "But no one says, 'Where is God my Maker, who gives strength in the night?'" (Job 35:10).

The text of Acts makes sure to note that "the prisoners were listening to them" as Paul and Silas prayed and sang hymns. They were not just startled from their sleep by the noises coming from the inner cell. They were truly "listening" with interest and amazement at these joyful and trusting invocations. The inmates in the other parts of the jail had probably never heard such words and melodies echoing from within a Roman prison, and they must have listened with wonder and awe.

From that dark prison in Philippi to jail cells throughout the world, people pay attention with great interest when Christians face adversity. Whether that hardship be sickness, the loss of a loved one, or unjust persecution, nonbelievers watch to see if faith is genuine. They want to see if the Christians believe what they say they believe. Many thousands of servants of Jesus Christ, during times of persecution, have sung from their prison cells, and they continue to sing today. Imagine the witness their melodic prayer offers to those around them. When prisoners sing hymns to God in prison, jailers and other prisoners listen well.

Paul and Silas had no idea an earthquake was coming that night. They weren't singing because they were going to be set free. They were living a joyful life of prayer and thanksgiving despite their circumstances. In spite of the bars and chains, they were the freest men in Philippi. Later, when Paul prepared his letter to the Philippian church, he wrote, "Rejoice in the Lord always; again I say, Rejoice" (Phil 4:4). He had already modeled for them the way to live such an always-rejoicing life.

Reflection and discussion

- What led the jailer to ask Paul and Silas, "What must I do to be saved?"

- Am I offering prayers and hymns to God in the midst of my adversities today?

- How does this episode encourage the reader to consider the meaning of genuine freedom and to ponder who is truly free?

Prayer

Risen Lord, whether I am well fed or hungry, satisfied or distressed, you offer me contentment in all circumstances. I can do all things and rejoice always because you are the source of my strength and my peace.

SUGGESTIONS FOR FACILITATORS, GROUP SESSION 5

1. Welcome group members and ask if anyone has any questions, announcements, or requests.

2. You may want to pray this prayer as a group:

   God of heaven and earth, you have cast away darkness from our world through the light of your Son, made flesh among us. Your holy witnesses— Mary, Zechariah, Simeon, Paul, Silas, and hosts of angels—have sung your praises for fulfilling the promises of your covenant. Lift up our hearts as we seek to live in the freedom you desire for us and to worship you in holiness all our days. May we express in melody and song our thankfulness for all you have done from generation to generation.

3. Ask one or more of the following questions:
   - What most intrigued you from this week's study?
   - How do the music and songs of Scripture encourage me to pray in new ways?

4. Discuss lessons 19 through 24. Choose one or more of the questions for reflection and discussion from each lesson to talk over as a group.

5. Ask the group members to name one thing they have most appreciated about the way the group has worked during this Bible study. Ask group members to discuss any changes they might suggest in the way the group works in future studies.

6. Invite group members to complete lessons 25 through 30 on their own during the six days before the next meeting. They should write out their own answers to the questions as preparation for next week's session.

7. Discuss with group members ways in which studying the music of the Bible could enhance their worship of God.

8. Conclude by praying aloud together the prayer at the end of one of the lessons discussed. You may want to conclude the prayer by asking members to voice prayers of thanksgiving.

At the name of Jesus every knee should bend, in heaven and on earth and under the earth, and every tongue should confess that Jesus Christ is Lord. PHILIPPIANS 2:10–11

The Philippian Hymn to Christ

PHILIPPIANS 2:5–11 *⁵Let the same mind be in you that was in Christ Jesus,*
⁶who, though he was in the form of God,
did not regard equality with God
as something to be exploited,
⁷but emptied himself,
taking the form of a slave,
being born in human likeness.
And being found in human form,
⁸he humbled himself
and became obedient to the point of death—
even death on a cross.
⁹Therefore God also highly exalted him
and gave him the name
that is above every name,
¹⁰so that at the name of Jesus
every knee should bend,
in heaven and on earth and under the earth,
¹¹and every tongue should confess
that Jesus Christ is Lord,
to the glory of God the Father.

The hymns contained in the various New Testament letters stand out from their context by their poetic and rhythmic nature. These early Christian songs, written within the church's first few decades, offer profound understandings of Christ's identity and mission. These hymns, in addition to the psalms and canticles of the Jewish tradition, were chanted in the liturgical worship of the Christian communities as they developed throughout the Roman world. Like all biblical music, they offered praise and thanks to God, commemorated the events of salvation, and reinforced the memorization of catechetical lessons. After singing these hymns in the Sunday Eucharist, believers would find themselves humming these melodies and repeating the lyrics throughout the week as they went about their business.

Whether this hymn to Christ was chosen by Paul from among the songs he knew or whether he wrote it himself, it expresses the message he sought to convey to the Philippians. Writing to a community divided by selfish ambition and self-interest, he sought to unite them by presenting Jesus Christ as a model for their behavior. The chant offers a profound theological meditation on what Jesus has come to do and the humility of his life, while also urging Paul's hearers to assimilate Christ's way of thinking (verse 5).

The hymn itself is clearly divided into two even parts, expressing a pattern of descending and ascending. Maybe it was sung at baptisms to express the sacramental dying and rising to new life. In the first part, Christ is the subject, and it expresses his humbling himself (verses 6–8); in the second, God is the subject, and it conveys God's exalting Jesus and giving him the name above every name (verses 9–11). The entire hymn consists of six stanzas of three lines each. This pattern is broken by one important exception: "even death on a cross" adds an extra line to the third stanza. This stark phrase was perhaps added by Paul to the existing hymn to emphasize the absolute depth to which Christ's humiliation descends and to anticipate the wonder of God's lifting this crucified slave to be the universal Lord.

The composer begins by expressing the preexistence of Christ prior to his life on earth. Although the Son was eternally equal to God the Father, he did not treat his divine status as an opportunity for self-exaltation (verse 6). Rather he became a human being, emptying himself of the majesty and privilege that belong to him as divine (verse 7). The one who was in "the form of

God," a status Roman citizens ascribed to the emperor, then took "the form of a slave," the very bottom of the social scale in Roman society. The one who "emptied himself" of divinity also "humbled himself" further, becoming "obedient to the point of death" (verse 8). This self-emptying in the incarnation and self-humbling in his human life culminated in the most humiliating suffering and death possible, the dreadful Roman execution reserved only for noncitizen criminals and slaves, "death on a cross."

From the rock bottom of human existence comes a complete reversal. The humiliated one is glorified (verse 9). Christ is now, in his human and divine nature, exalted and enthroned as Lord of all creation. The stanzas carefully build up to the climactic proclamation that "Jesus Christ is Lord," the earliest creedal confession among the Gentile Christians. He is Lord over every power in creation, "in heaven and on earth and under the earth" (verse 10). There is no place in the universe, no created being, beyond the reach of Christ's redeeming action. "Every knee" and "every tongue" refer to every personal being in the cosmos. For the Philippians and other churches that often promoted themselves rather than their crucified and risen Christ, this hymn not only exalts Jesus as Lord but sounds a judgment upon the kind of triumphalism that abandons the way of humble service.

Reflection and discussion

- Since God could have saved humanity in any number of ways, why is it significant that the central event in the drama of salvation is an act of humble service and self-giving?

- Why does the church need to sing and remember this descent and ascent of Christ, the central event that begets, nourishes, and matures the community of faith?

- What does it mean practically for me to humble myself like Christ?

- What melodic movement and musical dynamics would best express the message of this hymn?

Prayer

Crucified Lord, who emptied yourself of glory and became obedient unto death, help me to imitate your humility, share in your suffering, and know the power of your resurrection.

He is the beginning, the firstborn from the dead, so that he might come to have first place in everything. For in him all the fullness of God was pleased to dwell. COLOSSIANS 1:18–19

The Colossian Hymn to Christ

COLOSSIANS 1:15–20 ¹⁵*He is the image of the invisible God, the firstborn of all creation;* ¹⁶*for in him all things in heaven and on earth were created, things visible and invisible, whether thrones or dominions or rulers or powers—all things have been created through him and for him.* ¹⁷*He himself is before all things, and in him all things hold together.* ¹⁸*He is the head of the body, the church; he is the beginning, the firstborn from the dead, so that he might come to have first place in everything.* ¹⁹*For in him all the fullness of God was pleased to dwell,* ²⁰*and through him God was pleased to reconcile to himself all things, whether on earth or in heaven, by making peace through the blood of his cross.*

This hymn of the cosmic Christ is distinguished by its lofty style and unique vocabulary from the more prosaic texts surrounding it. It expounds the universal foundation for the experiences of Paul and the Colossian Christians discussed in the letter. The hymn is composed of two parallel stanzas: the first, elaborating the role of Christ in creation (verses 15–17), and the second, developing his role in the new creation (verses 18–20). Two corresponding titles of Christ are spotlighted in each stanza: in the first, he is named "the firstborn of all creation," and in the second, he is called "the firstborn from the dead."

The hymn begins by describing the preeminence of the Son of God, first by describing him as "the image of the invisible God" (verse 15). The Greek word here for image is *eikon*, from which we receive the word "icon." To look upon Jesus Christ is to see the face of the eternal, invisible God. Second, calling him the "firstborn," the composer draws upon the rich biblical understanding of the firstborn son in a family. The firstborn is distinguished as both the first to be born to his parents and the one who receives the greatest privileges and inheritance. Applying this title to the Son, the hymn declares Christ as the firstborn in both senses: the universe was created "through him and for him" (verse 16). He is the one through whom the Father created everything from the beginning and the one who is the heir of all things.

The comprehensive and universal scope of the hymn is characterized by its repetition of the words "all things." The entire world, in all its beauty, complexity, and mystery, has been fashioned through Christ and for Christ. "All things" include everything "in heaven and on earth" and "things visible and invisible"; that is, the physical universe, including the people, places, and things distinguishable through our senses, and the spiritual, angelic creatures, which include the thrones, dominions, rulers, and powers. The eternal Son was not himself created, but he is "before all things" as the mediator through whom all things were created (verse 17). And he continues to give order to the universe as the one in whom "all things" hold together.

The second stanza moves from the cosmic to the ecclesial, from the universe to the church (verse 18). The body, of which Jesus Christ is the head, is the worldwide church, the church both in heaven and on earth. Just as the Son is the beginning of creation, its source and sustainer, so he is the "beginning" of his church. As "the firstborn from the dead," he is the first to pass through human existence and the defeat of death into a new and glorious life. He is the beginning, source, sustainer, and heir of the new creation.

In Jesus Christ, as the new and living temple, dwells "the fullness" of divinity (verse 19). And through this divine fullness, with all its creative and redeeming power, God has reconciled not just persons but "all things," whether on earth or in heaven (verse 20). Since the whole created world shares in the disorder and corruption caused by human sin, so all creation will be restored to its full beauty and harmony. This "making peace," reestablishing the splendor of creation and the goodness of humanity, is accomplished in Christ "through the blood of his cross," healing the relationship between God and the world.

Reflection and discussion

- How do the titles "firstborn of all creation" and "firstborn from the dead" enrich my understanding of Jesus Christ?

- Why does the hymn continually repeat the phrases "in him," "through him," and "for him"?

- How does the hymn's repetition of "all things" expand my appreciation of the breadth of God's saving will?

Prayer

Firstborn of all creation, the entire cosmos bears your imprint because all things came into being through you and for you. Through the blood of your cross and your resurrection, redeem your creation and reconcile heaven and earth for your glory.

For Christ also suffered for sins once for all, the righteous for the unrighteous, in order to bring you to God. He was put to death in the flesh, but made alive in the spirit. 1 PETER 3:18

Hymn Fragments in Peter's Letter

1 PETER 2:21–25 ²¹*For to this you have been called, because Christ also suffered for you, leaving you an example, so that you should follow in his steps.*

> ²²*"He committed no sin,*
> *and no deceit was found in his mouth."*

²³*When he was abused, he did not return abuse; when he suffered, he did not threaten; but he entrusted himself to the one who judges justly.* ²⁴*He himself bore our sins in his body on the cross, so that, free from sins, we might live for righteousness; by his wounds you have been healed.* ²⁵*For you were going astray like sheep, but now you have returned to the shepherd and guardian of your souls.*

1 PETER 3:18–22 ¹⁸*For Christ also suffered for sins once for all, the righteous for the unrighteous, in order to bring you to God. He was put to death in the flesh, but made alive in the spirit,* ¹⁹*in which also he went and made a proclamation to the spirits in prison,* ²⁰*who in former times did not obey, when God waited patiently in the days of Noah, during the building of the ark, in which a few, that is, eight persons, were saved through water.* ²¹*And baptism, which this prefigured, now saves you—not as a removal of dirt from the body, but as an appeal to God for a good conscience, through the resurrection of Jesus Christ,* ²²*who has gone into heaven and is at the right hand of God, with angels, authorities, and powers made subject to him.*

Whether these hymnic passages from Peter's letter are his own composition or fragments of earlier hymns that the author extracted for his teaching, they are meant to instruct the hearers on how to follow Christ more closely. The letter is addressed to persecuted, suffering Christians, and both passages begin with the words "Christ also suffered" (2:21; 3:18), indicating that the way of Jesus serves as "an example" for the life of his disciples. This emphasis on suffering in Peter's letter is remarkable when we consider that Peter in the gospels rejected any thought of a suffering Messiah when Jesus announced the way ahead (Mark 8:32). But in the intervening years, Peter clearly grew to understand the necessity of suffering for our redemption. Here he shows that the suffering of Jesus is not just an inspiration for the Christian, but a precise pattern to be imitated, a way to "follow in his steps" (2:21), "in order to bring you to God" (3:18).

Peter weaves together a tapestry of verses drawn from the prophetic passages on the Suffering Servant (Isaiah 53:4–12), offering us a profound summary of Christ's saving work. Although he was free from any sin or deception, thus deserving no punishment at all, he was insulted and abused (2:22–23). Yet he did not strike back, return the abuse, or seek vengeance on his persecutors. Instead, he gave himself into the hands of the Father.

Although humanity was weighed down by sin, Jesus Christ took this burden upon himself when he offered his life as a sacrifice that resulted in the forgiveness of our sins (2:24). Through his innocent suffering, we are now freed to "live for righteousness," that is, to live a new life of holiness in union with God. By his wounds we have been healed. The Suffering Servant, who gave his life for us, is now our "shepherd and guardian," leading our way into increasingly fuller life (2:25). Christ's redemptive suffering is a unique event for the world's salvation, an action that we could never have done for ourselves. Yet we cannot just look upon him from a safe distance. Peter calls us to walk in Christ's steps and imitate him in our own circumstances, persevering in the sufferings of life.

In the next passage, Peter includes what seems to be part of a baptismal hymn, proclaiming the saving work of Christ, the goal of which is to bring us into the presence of God (3:18). He professes the innocent suffering of Jesus, whose crucifixion provides the single sacrifice for sins that will never need repeating. "He was put to death in the flesh," that is, in the realm of his earthly, human life, "but made alive in the spirit," in his glorified state of existence.

This paschal mystery of Christ—his passion, death, resurrection, and glorification—is the saving work into which the baptized believer is incorporated.

One aspect of Christ's ascent from the grave to glory is his "proclamation to the spirits in prison," those angelic beings who led humanity into an ever-greater wickedness at the time of Noah (3:19–20). Because Christ's triumph is complete, these spirits no longer have power over humanity. Christ has redeemed the world from the powers of evil and death, giving humanity new hope through its new birth in Christ. As God rescued Noah and his family from the evil world by means of water, God saves faithful believers by means of the waters of baptism (3:21).

The divine power that raised Jesus Christ is the same power that purifies our conscience and transforms us through baptism. As we step into the way of Christ, we cannot head off in any other direction than the direction he took: to the cross, through the grave, and onward to glory. The past suffering of Christ is the present condition of believers, while the present glory of Christ is the future glory of those who follow in his footsteps.

Reflection and discussion

• How might Peter suggest that I imitate Jesus Christ by following in his steps?

• What is the meaning of Peter's words, "By his wounds you have been healed"?

- Both passages begin with the words "Christ also suffered." How did Peter learn the value of suffering?

- In what situations today do Christians face unjust suffering? What advice and consolation does Peter offer to them?

- What does Peter tell me about the effects of baptism upon my life?

Prayer

Lord God, through my baptism you have rescued me from the powers of evil and death, given me a new birth in Christ, and given me hope for future glory. Lead me to follow in the way of Jesus, through his cross to a liberated and transformed life.

"Worthy is the Lamb that was slaughtered to receive power and wealth and wisdom and might and honor and glory and blessing!"
REVELATION 5:12

New Song of Praise to the Lamb

REVELATION 5:6–14 ⁶*Then I saw between the throne and the four living creatures and among the elders a Lamb standing as if it had been slaughtered, having seven horns and seven eyes, which are the seven spirits of God sent out into all the earth.* ⁷*He went and took the scroll from the right hand of the one who was seated on the throne.* ⁸*When he had taken the scroll, the four living creatures and the twenty-four elders fell before the Lamb, each holding a harp and golden bowls full of incense, which are the prayers of the saints.* ⁹*They sing a new song:*

"You are worthy to take the scroll
and to open its seals,
for you were slaughtered and by your blood you ransomed for God
saints from every tribe and language and people and nation;
¹⁰*you have made them to be a kingdom and priests serving our God,*
and they will reign on earth."

¹¹*Then I looked, and I heard the voice of many angels surrounding the throne and the living creatures and the elders; they numbered myriads of myriads and thousands of thousands,* ¹²*singing with full voice,*

"Worthy is the Lamb that was slaughtered
to receive power and wealth and wisdom and might
and honor and glory and blessing!"

¹³*Then I heard every creature in heaven and on earth and under the earth and in
the sea, and all that is in them, singing,*

> *"To the one seated on the throne and to the Lamb*
> *be blessing and honor and glory and might*
> *forever and ever!"*

¹⁴*And the four living creatures said, "Amen!" And the elders fell down and
worshipped.*

The music of the Bible concludes with the dramatic visions received by
John while exiled on the island of Patmos. The author received these
visions "while in the spirit on the Lord's day," probably while partici-
pating in the church's eucharistic liturgy. Written during a time of intense persecution of the church, the Book of Revelation seeks to bring encouragement
and hope to Christians. The many hymns throughout the work draw together
the heavenly liturgy and the worshipping church on earth, assuring believers
that the kingdom of God is present with us, now and forever.

This scene introduces "a Lamb standing as if it had been slaughtered," an
image of Jesus Christ, slain in his passion and glorified in his resurrection, triumphant but bearing the marks of his sacrifice. The author draws upon a rich
heritage of Israelite and Christian imagery in depicting Christ as God's Lamb.
Already in the first book of the Bible, when Isaac asked his father, Abraham,
"Where is the lamb for the sacrifice," Abraham replied, "God himself will provide the lamb (Gen 22:8). All of salvation history is really a waiting for this
Lamb that God would give to his people. In the story of Exodus, the Israelites
sacrificed the lamb of Passover on the night of their liberation. The blood of
the lamb on their doorposts freed them from the final destructive plague so
they could journey to the land promised to them.

In explaining the meaning of Christ's sacrifice, the early Christians looked
to the Scriptures of Israel. Isaiah had described the Suffering Servant, a figure
who suffered vicariously for God's people, as afflicted and wounded, "like a
lamb that is led to the slaughter (Isa 53:7). John's gospel sums up the ancient
sacrificial images of the Old Testament when he calls Jesus "the Lamb of
God who takes away the sin of the world (John 1:29, 36), and Paul uses the
same imagery when he calls Jesus the "paschal lamb" who has been sacri-

ficed (1 Cor 5:7). "The Lamb" appears twenty-eight times in the Book of Revelation, always as a rich verbal icon of Christ.

The scene presents God "seated on the throne" of heaven, worshipped by "four living creatures," representing all the living beings of creation. Resembling a lion, an ox, a human being, and a flying eagle, they symbolize what is noblest, strongest, wisest, and swiftest in creation (4:7). The twenty-four elders, representing the twelve patriarchs of Israel and the twelve apostles, wear white robes and crowns of gold. As God holds the scroll, containing the divine, redemptive plan for the world, only the Lamb is declared worthy to break its seals and open the scroll. Christ alone may exercise the Father's reign and execute the divine plan. As the Lamb receives the scroll from the right hand of God, the heavenly assembly falls down in adoration, as the worship of God becomes the worship of the Lamb (verses 7–8).

The celestial beings, each holding a harp and a bowl of incense, sing to the Lamb (verse 9). The music of the harps, the sight and smell of rising incense, and the song of praise resemble the worship of God in the earthly temple and the liturgy of the church. The "new song" celebrates the worthiness of the Lamb, the saving work of the Lamb, and its effects for the followers of the Lamb. The blood of his paschal sacrifice "ransomed" those enslaved by sin and brought them into his church, gathered "from every tribe and language and people and nation." Christ has made them saints, "a kingdom and priests serving our God" (verse 10). All the promises God made to the people through the Torah and prophets of Israel are being fulfilled. The death of Christ has become his final victory over evil and has established his worldwide church as a royal and priestly kingdom.

The hymn crescendos as the choir is joined by the voices of countless angels (verses 11–12). In this majestic scene, the angels surrounding the throne acclaim the Lamb "with full voice." They acclaim him as worthy to receive a sevenfold praise. First, they acclaim Christ's attributes: power, wealth, wisdom, and might. Then, they celebrate the worship due to him as a result: honor, glory, and blessing. Indeed, the divine Lamb is worthy of the same worship as God.

Finally, the hymn surges to its climax as every created being in the universe joins in the heavenly worship (verses 13–14). They offer praise "to the one seated on the throne and to the Lamb," that is, to the Father and the

Son together. Indeed, the cosmos worships Jesus Christ, who is our sovereign Lord, worthy of supreme worship forever.

Reflection and discussion

- In what sense is the liturgy we celebrate on the Lord's Day a participation in the heavenly liturgy?

- Why is the Lamb of God such a traditional image of Christ in the church's liturgical worship?

- What does it matter that the angels, saints, and every created being in the universe praise God with me? How could a greater awareness of this reality enhance my worship?

Prayer

Lamb of God, who takes away the sins of the world, you are indeed worthy to receive honor, glory, and blessing. May I praise your victory on the cross and worship you forever with all the creatures of heaven and earth.

The nations raged, but your wrath has come, and the time
for judging the dead, for rewarding your servants, the prophets
and saints and all who fear your name." REVELATION 11:18

Hymn to Divine Judgment and Triumph

REVELATION 11:15–18 ¹⁵*Then the seventh angel blew his trumpet, and there were loud voices in heaven, saying,*

"The kingdom of the world has become the kingdom of our Lord
    and of his Messiah,
and he will reign forever and ever."
¹⁶*Then the twenty-four elders who sit on their thrones before God fell on their faces and worshiped God,* ¹⁷*singing,*
"We give you thanks, Lord God Almighty,
    who are and who were,
for you have taken your great power
    and begun to reign.
¹⁸*The nations raged,*
    but your wrath has come,
    and the time for judging the dead,
for rewarding your servants, the prophets
    and saints and all who fear your name,
    both small and great,
and for destroying those who destroy the earth."

REVELATION 12:7–12 *⁷And war broke out in heaven; Michael and his angels fought against the dragon. The dragon and his angels fought back, ⁸but they were defeated, and there was no longer any place for them in heaven. ⁹The great dragon was thrown down, that ancient serpent, who is called the Devil and Satan, the deceiver of the whole world—he was thrown down to the earth, and his angels were thrown down with him.*

¹⁰Then I heard a loud voice in heaven, proclaiming,
"Now have come the salvation and the power
and the kingdom of our God
and the authority of his Messiah,
for the accuser of our comrades has been thrown down,
who accuses them day and night before our God.
¹¹But they have conquered him by the blood of the Lamb
and by the word of their testimony,
for they did not cling to life even in the face of death.
¹²Rejoice then, you heavens
and those who dwell in them!
But woe to the earth and the sea,
for the devil has come down to you
with great wrath,
because he knows that his time is short!"

Throughout the Bible, trumpets are blown to summon Israel to battle, to call Israel to repentance, to install new kings, and to convene worshippers for pilgrimages and solemn feasts. God's people associate sounding trumpets with alarm, terror, praise, and joy. In the Book of Revelation, the seventh trumpet sounds the final climax of God's triumph over evil and the coming of God's kingdom. Instead of more plagues and woes as brought by the first six trumpets, we are surprised to hear an outburst of rejoicing in heaven. The symphony of sound is a victory celebration: "The kingdom of the world has become the kingdom of our Lord and of his Messiah, and he will reign forever and ever" (11:15). The kingdom is no longer "of the world" but now and forevermore is "of our Lord and of his Messiah." There is an inseparable unity between the Father and the Son; the kingdom belongs to both equally. This is the messianic kingdom that Jewish and New Testament expectation throughout the Bible has anticipated.

The twenty-four elders then sing of the establishment of God's reign (11:16–18). The heavenly scene reflects the inner reality and the final outcome of ongoing earthly events. The victory of God over evil has been won. It is time for the dead to be judged and for the faithful to be rewarded. As seen from the viewpoint of eternity, God's purposes are already fulfilled in the triumph of Christ on the cross. The kingdom of the world has indeed become the kingdom of God, where he will reign with the Lamb forever. The ultimate goal presented with the seven trumpets is not destruction but the liberation of all humanity and the whole earth from oppressive and destructive powers. This is the blessed hope that John's vision places before us.

The next heavenly vision depicts the cosmic battle between God's saving will and the forces of evil (12:7). The battle in heaven is fought between the archangel Michael and his angels and the dragon and his angels. In the Old Testament, Michael is the protector of God's people, the patron angel of Israel. The dragon represents the vast reservoir of evil by which the world is threatened and from which we cannot deliver ourselves. By identifying the dragon with Satan, the devil, and the ancient serpent (12:9), the author intends to symbolize all the forces that seek to ensnare humanity, beginning in the garden of Eden and continuing throughout the biblical narrative.

As proclaimed in the heavenly song that interprets the action, the expulsion of the dragon from heaven is the result of both the atoning death of Christ and the witness of his followers (12:10–11). The blood of Christian martyrdom flows together with the "the blood of the Lamb." Their "testimony" attests that "they did not cling to life even in the face of death." Although the devil and his angels are already defeated in the transcendent world, they have been cast down to this world, frustrated and angry (12:12). This explains why the church's struggle has not ended. The battle continues on earth, but the power of Satan has been broken. His influence is limited and his days are numbered.

Reflection and discussion

- In the midst of life's struggles, do I believe that Christ reigns over the world and promises me victory?

- How does the church participate in the Lamb's conquest of the powers of the dragon?

- What are some indications that Satan and his angels have been cast down to earth where the battle continues?

Prayer

We give you thanks, Lord God Almighty, for you reign forever with Christ. I know that the power of the Lamb has conquered the powers of evil. Strengthen your church as we await the return of your Son in glory.

The voice I heard was like the sound of harpists playing on their harps, and they sing a new song before the throne and before the four living creatures and before the elders. REVELATION 14:2–3

Hymn of Adoration before the Throne

REVELATION 14:1–3 ¹*Then I looked, and there was the Lamb, standing on Mount Zion! And with him were one hundred forty-four thousand who had his name and his Father's name written on their foreheads. ²And I heard a voice from heaven like the sound of many waters and like the sound of loud thunder; the voice I heard was like the sound of harpists playing on their harps, ³and they sing a new song before the throne and before the four living creatures and before the elders. No one could learn that song except the one hundred forty-four thousand who have been redeemed from the earth.*

REVELATION 15:2–4 ²*And I saw what appeared to be a sea of glass mixed with fire, and those who had conquered the beast and its image and the number of its name, standing beside the sea of glass with harps of God in their hands. ³And they sing the song of Moses, the servant of God, and the song of the Lamb:*
  "Great and amazing are your deeds,
    Lord God the Almighty!
  Just and true are your ways,
    King of the nations!
  ⁴*Lord, who will not fear*
    and glorify your name?
  For you alone are holy.

All nations will come
and worship before you,
for your judgments have been revealed."

The Lamb stands in triumph on Mount Zion with the 144,000: twelve thousand from each of the twelve tribes of the restored Israel. They are the church, those who have remained true to Christ through the great adversity. They bear the names of the Lamb and the Father on their fore-heads, indicating to whom they belong, and participate in the joyful victory (14:1). They know that God will protect those who bear his name.

After John "looked" and saw the vision of the Lamb and his triumphant followers, he "heard" a voice from heaven (14:2). He compared the voice to rushing water, pealing thunder, and the music of harps—combining images of power and gentleness. The "new song" sung before God's throne celebrates God's redeeming action, the Lamb's triumph, and God's judgment of the earth (14:3). A "new song," throughout the Book of Psalms, describes a hymn of praise for the fact that God has delivered his people and a call for them to place their trust completely in God (Ps 33:3; 40:3; 96:1; 98:1; 144:9; 149:1). This song of victory seems to be the same "new song" sung at John's first vision of the Lamb, a scene that also includes the four living creatures and the elders before God's throne (5:9–14). Since this "new song" is the divine worship in heaven, the 144,000—those "who have been redeemed from the earth"—must learn the hymn in order to sing with the choirs of heaven.

The next vision depicts the church triumphant, those who had conquered the beastly powers through the blood of the Lamb, standing before the throne of God with harps in their hands (15:2). They sing both the "song of Moses"—Israel's song of victory over their oppressors (Exod 15; Deut 32)—and the "song of the Lamb"—the new hymn of God's victory over the power of their persecutors (15:3). The song of the Lamb contains numerous refer-ences to the Scriptures of Israel, building upon the song of Moses and other hymns of victory. The first stanza describes God's "deeds," which are "great and amazing." The second describes God's "ways," which are "just and true."

The next stanza presents a rhetorical question: "Lord, who will not fear and glorify your name?" (15:4). This incomparability of God is the theme of the remainder of the hymn. This builds on the question asked in Moses' Song of the Sea: "Who is like you, O Lord, among the gods? Who is like you, majestic in holiness, awesome in splendor, doing wonders?" (Exod 15:11). The song of the Lamb concludes by addressing God with three reasons why all should "fear and glorify" him: first, "You alone are holy"; second, "All nations will come and worship you"; and third, "Your judgments have been revealed."

Like the other hymns of Revelation, the song of the Lamb was sung in the liturgy of the early church. This heavenly song is given to the church now on earth as an encouragement to trust in God despite the temporary sufferings of our lives. When we pray and worship God with the angels and saints, we anticipate the life that will be ours forever. The Lord God, who is "the Almighty" and the "King of the nations," calls us now to sing of our confident trust in the victory of the Lamb and of our hope in the abundant life to come.

Reflection and discussion

- Why are the song of Moses and the song of the Lamb sung together by the assembly worshipping in heaven?

- How does singing hymns from the viewpoint of heaven help me understand the reality of my life on earth?

Prayer

King of the nations, you alone are holy, your deeds are great and amazing, and your ways are just and true. Deliver me from bondage and bring me to experience the fullness of your salvation.

SUGGESTIONS FOR FACILITATORS, GROUP SESSION 6

1. Welcome group members and make any final announcements or requests.

2. You may want to pray this prayer as a group:
   Lord Jesus Christ, although you are the firstborn of all creation, and all things were created through you and for you, you emptied yourself of glory and became obedient even unto death on a cross. As the Lamb of God, you offered your life in sacrifice for the sins of the world, rescued us from the powers of evil and death, and gave us a new birth and hope for future glory. May your church give you glory and honor, imitate your suffering with the hope of victory, and worship you forever with all the creatures of heaven and earth.

3. Ask one or more of the following questions:
   - How has this study of the music of the Bible deepened your life in Christ?
   - In what way has this study challenged you the most?

4. Discuss lessons 25 through 30. Choose one or more of the questions for reflection and discussion from each lesson to discuss as a group.

5. Ask the group if they would like to study another in the *Threshold Bible Study* series. Discuss the topic and dates, and make a decision among those interested. Ask the group members to suggest people they would like to invite to participate in the next study series.

6. Ask the group to discuss the insights that stand out most from this study over the past six weeks.

7. Conclude by praying aloud the following prayer or another of your own choosing:
   Holy Spirit of the living God, you inspired the writers of the Scriptures, and you have guided our study during these weeks. Continue to deepen our love for the word of God in the holy Scriptures, and draw us more deeply into the heart of Jesus. Thank you for your merciful, gracious, steadfast, and faithful love.

TWENTY-THIRD PUBLICATIONS

Dear Friend of Twenty-Third Publications,

The author of the enclosed new book has asked us to send you a review copy. We hope you enjoy it and would appreciate your help in getting the word out about it.

Thank you very much!

Kerry
Kerry.Moriarty@Bayard-inc.com
800-321-0411 ext. 813

FOR MORE INFORMATION ON THIS BOOK
OR OTHER GREAT TITLES, PLEASE VISIT OUR WEBSITE AT
WWW.TWENTYTHIRDPUBLICATIONS.COM